Cooking Backyard

12 Techniques and 150
Recipes For Fabulous
Outdoor Cooking

to Backcountry

John Rittel AND **Lori Rittel,** M.S., R.D.

D1602108

RIVERBEND
PUBLISHING

P.O. Box 5833
Helena, MT 59604
1-866-787-2363
www.riverbendpublishing.com

CONTENTS

ACKNOWLEDGEMENTS

We would like to thank everyone who helped us make this dream a reality by digging pits, testing recipes, reading, making suggestions and offering advice. A special thanks to Gail Johnson, Jeri Rittel, Julian Calabrese, Colet Bartow, Paddy Ferriter, Margaret Jenkins and of course, Chris Cauble and Riverbend Publishing for taking this dream to fruition.

Along with those who helped and supported us during the creation and completion of this book, we must thank our parents, Tag and Lyla Rittel, who raised us on the family ranch and taught us to love and respect the outdoors. Along with frequent backyard cooking, we spent countless days and nights of our childhood camping in the mountains on the ranch or packing horses into the backcountry. After cooking outdoors throughout the years and experiencing everything from deep pit barbecue to "fish frys" along the creek to cooking steaks in the fireplace because it rained us out of the yard, we found it natural to use our lifetime experience to present and share these wonderful cooking methods through a book.

INTRODUCTION

We grew up on our family ranch in the Rocky Mountains where we spent more time outdoors than indoors. Whether hiking, camping, horseback riding, entertaining, or just having fun, enjoying good food cooked over an open fire was always one of the most satisfying and memorable experiences, especially when shared with family and friends. Through the years we have perfected a variety of simple, interesting techniques—some very old, some relatively new—that transform routine meal preparation into unforgettable outdoor cooking.

Instead of the standard "boil in the pot and fry in the pan" cookery, we focus on exceptional, ingenious, and sometimes outright primitive cooking methods that vibrantly enhance flavor and preserve the natural texture and succulence of foods. Most chapters explain a particular cooking technique, including its history and how it works. This information is followed by a "how to" section and field-tested recipes.

Some techniques will require your full attention while others will allow you to enjoy unrelated activities as the food cooks. You may want to first practice some recipes and procedures at home before taking them to the woods. Whether used in the deepest wilderness or in the most urban backyard, these cooking methods create unique, entertaining, and, most importantly, gastronomically rewarding experiences of their own.

CHAPTER 1

FOODS & FUNDAMENTALS

For most camping trips, freeze-dried foods and processed "meals-in-a-bag" are not necessary. Wholesome foods and proper cooking techniques make outdoor meals simple, inexpensive, healthy, and flavorful. We hope this book will encourage you to experience the fun of cooking outdoors.

The recipes in this book have been tested for the various cooking techniques. Once you learn the techniques you may want to try your home favorites. Most any recipe can be adapted to one or more of these methods.

RECIPE ABBREVIATIONS USED IN THIS BOOK

t	teaspoon	T	tablespoon
fl	fluid	oz	ounce
pkg	package	pt	pint
qt	quart	gal	gallon
lb	pound	°	degrees in Fahrenheit

FOOD SAFETY

Foods should be kept cold (40°F or below), or hot (over 140°). Temperatures between 40° and 140° are the "danger zone," the perfect temperature for bacterial growth. Potentially hazardous foods (meats, cooked foods, leftovers, etc.) should be kept out of the danger zone as much as possible.

At the grocery store, pick up cold foods like meat, fish, poultry, and frozen foods just before checking out. Put packages of meat, poultry, and fish into plastic bags and keep them separate from other groceries. For the drive home, pack cold and frozen items in the coolest part of the car. If it is warm and you have more than a twenty-minute drive, bring a cooler with ice for the perishable foods. Once home, first unpack the meat, poultry, and fish and refrigerate them immediately. Freeze any cuts that you don't plan to cook within the next day or two.

For your camping trip, pack dry good and dishes first. Pack plenty of clean utensils and plates because you need separate utensils and platters for raw meat and for cooked meat. Be sure to pack tongs, heavy gloves (for handling wood), a disposable lighter (the long-necked barbecue lighter is best), and pump-type spray bottles for cooking oil and for water (to cool fire/coals if they get too hot). Also, pack plenty of heavy-duty aluminum foil.

Minimize weight and space before leaving home. Take everything out of the original packaging and put it in plastic bags or smaller containers that are more easily packed. Ground meat can be mixed with seasonings and put in a plastic zipper bag. For an instant burger put one serving of ground meat in a sandwich bags and smash it flat. Put condiments in squeeze bottles. Glass and plastic jars take up too much space in a cooler.

Pour juices into empty plastic soda or water bottles. Leave room at the top for expansion during freezing. Recycle empty bags from inside boxed wines; remove the rubber spigots and re-fill with juice, tea, or water. The bags take up less space in coolers and can be frozen to keep your cooler cold. As the bag thaws, you have a fresh, cold beverage. Freeze fresh herbs in small zipper bags to take along—fresh has a much better flavor than dried.

Use an insulated cooler with sufficient ice or ice packs. It is best to have one cooler for frozen foods and extra ice, another cooler for beverages (this cooler will likely be opened most often), and a third cooler for foods that need to be kept cool but not frozen. You can keep the frozen foods for at least a week by placing dry ice wrapped in brown paper in the bottom of the cooler. Lay cubed ice over the dry ice to prevent packages from freezing together.

Pack cold and frozen items just before leaving home. Transport your coolers in the coolest part of your vehicle and avoid opening the lids too often, as this allows cold air out and warm air in. If you pack your coolers according to how your meals are planned, with the items to be used first at the top, you will minimize the amount of time that you have the cooler open searching for what you need.

Before leaving home, try to find out if your camping area has drinking water. If not, bring enough water for food preparation, cleaning up, and drinking. Anti-bacterial wipes will help keep hands and equipment clean, particularly if you are in an area of limited water supply.

When you reach your campsite, store your coolers in a shady area on the ground. Only take out meat, fish, or poultry when you are ready to cook or defrost it. Frozen foods can be thawed out by moving them from the "freezing-cold" cooler to one of the "cold" coolers. Be sure meat is in a sealed package so its juices don't leak onto other foods. You may also thaw frozen, sealed packages by submerging them in cold water.

Meat, fish, and poultry are often marinated. Do this in the refrigerator at home or in a cooler at camp, not in the open air. If some of the marinade is to be used later as a sauce, set aside a portion of the marinade for that purpose; don't put raw meat, fish, or poultry in it. If you're short on marinade for sauce, you can use the marinade that was on the meat if you bring it to a full boil before serving it.

When cooking in the yard, it is fine to reduce grilling time by partially cooking food in the microwave or standard oven—provided you take it straight to the hot grill. Do not use this technique for camping. Never partially cook meat and then stop the cooking process to finish cooking later on.

Meat and poultry cooked on a grill will often brown very fast on the outside before the inside is properly cooked. A meat thermometer or probe is the best way to indicate doneness. Place the probe in the thickest part of meats, or the center of casseroles and other dishes, while being careful not to touch bones or the sides of containers.

Letting the meat "rest" for several minutes before being served allows the temperature to stabilize as heat moves from the hotter exterior to the cooler

interior. The interior temperature may continue to increase in temperature by 5 to 10° after being removed from the heat. To achieve a final temperature (level of doneness) that is precisely what you want, remove the meat from the heat 5 to 10° before it is "done" and let it rest.

The appropriate doneness temperature and the level of doneness are often hot topics of debate. Are you more inclined to worry about parasites and bacteria or taste and texture? The United States Department of Agriculture (USDA) and the Food and Drug Administration (FDA) do not recommend consuming meats that are cooked at less than 145° and they set the temperature even higher for other foods. For the purposes of safety, the following chart shows temperature gradations established by the FDA. Note that temperatures less than 145° are not recommended by the FDA.

Hold cooked foods at 140° or warmer (out of the danger zone) until served. Set cooked foods on the side of the grill rack or at the edge of the campfire. Do not leave finished food directly over the coals as it will continue to cook and may overcook and dry out. At home, cooked foods may be kept in a warm (200°) oven, in a chafing dish, slow cooker, or on a warming tray.

When possible, promptly refrigerate leftovers in shallow containers because they cool faster than deep pans. Discard any food left out at room (or ambient) temperature for more than two hours. In hot weather (90° and above), cooked food should never sit out for more than one hour.

SLOW COOKING FOODS SAFELY

Smoking is a slow-cooking process that is perfect for less tender cuts of meat such as ribs and shoulder cuts. To safely smoke foods, maintain smoker temperatures at 250-300° and check for doneness with a food thermometer to be certain the food has reached a safe internal temperature.

Slow cooking such as Dutch oven, deep-pit barbecue, and fireless cookery is great for camping because you can leave food unattended while you go off

GENERAL GUIDELINE FOR DONENESS

Food	Doneness	Internal Temperature (Degrees Fahrenheit)
Beef Brisket, Barbecued	Fully Cooked	210
Beef, Ground	Medium	160
Beef, Roast & Steaks	Rare	125-145*
	Medium-Rare	145-150
	Medium	150-165
	Medium-Well	165-170
	Well-Done	>170
Duck	Fully Cooked	165
Fish	Fully Cooked	145
Ham, Precooked	Fully Heated	140
Ham, Fresh	Fully Cooked	160
Hot Dogs	Fully Heated	165
Lamb Chops, Rack, or Roast	Rare	124-145*
	Medium-Rare	145-150
	Medium-Well	165-170
	Well-Done	>170
Leftovers	Thoroughly Reheated	165
Pork, Barbecued	Fully Cooked	180 to slice 190 to pull
Pork Chops	Medium-Rare	145-150
	Medium	150-165
	Medium-Well	165-170
	Well-Done	>170
Pork, Ground	Fully Cooked	160
Poultry, Whole, Leg, or Thighs	Fully Cooked	180
Poultry, Breast	Fully Cooked	170
Poultry, Ground	Fully Cooked	165
Sausage	Fully Cooked	160
Veal	Medium-Rare	145-150
	Medium	150-165
	Medium-Well	165-170
	Well-Done	>170
Venison, Elk	Fully Cooked	165

* The FDA recommends cooking meat to at least 145°

hiking or fishing. There are just a few important things to keep in mind to keep your slow-cooking method a safe method.

Be certain that all foods, especially previously frozen meats, poultry, and fish, are completely thawed before using in a slow-cooking process. This will help the food cook to the appropriate temperature. Adding frozen foods to the contents of a slow cooker will cause the entire contents to chill to unsafe temperatures (the danger zone) before the food has finished cooking. With any slow-cooking method, it is important that foods heat up quickly and that the proper heat is maintained for the required length of time. Choose recipes that have a high moisture content because the moisture helps the food heat rapidly. When removing food from any type of slow cooking process, make sure it is still steaming.

Pit roasting may require 6 to 12 hours or more. Actual cooking times are difficult to estimate and depend on the starting temperature of the pit, ambient temperatures, the thickness of meats, placement of food packages, and the total volume of foods being cooked. It is important to start with enough wood coals to generate sufficient heat to cook the food to desired doneness. Food may not fully cook if the starting temperature and heat volume are too low. In most earthen pits the food is buried too deeply for direct thermometer readings. In these instances a potato can be placed in an accessible area near the pit surface and used as an indicator for doneness (see Chapter 13).

SUBSTITUTIONS FOR HEALTHIER RECIPES

You can decrease the amount of fat, calories, sugar, and salt and/or increase the fiber in many of your favorite recipes quite easily.

To decrease total fat and calories of a recipe, reduce the fat or oil by one quarter to one third. For example, if a recipe calls for 1 cup of oil, use 2/3 cup instead. (Do not use this method for yeast breads and piecrusts).

Use vegetable oil instead of solid fats such as shortening, lard, and butter to lower trans-fatty acids (found in shortening) and cholesterol (found in lard and butter). Unsaturated vegetable oils from canola, peanuts, olive, flax, corn, safflower, and sunflower are heart healthy (as long as they have not been subjected to the process of hydrogenation, e.g. they have not been made solid or semi-solid). When substituting liquid oil for solid fats, use about 1/8 cup less. For example, if a recipe calls for 1/4 cup shortening (4 T), use 3 T oil instead.

In recipes calling for sour cream, substitute plain low fat or nonfat yogurt, buttermilk, or blended low-fat cottage cheese. You can cook with low fat or no-fat dairy products using skim or one- percent milk instead of whole milk or half & half. This can really cut calories and fat. If you want extra richness, try canned evaporated skim milk. It's thicker, like cream, but without the fat.

To cut back on sugar in baked goods and desserts, reduce the sugar by one quarter to one third but don't leave it out completely. Besides adding sweetness, sugar increases the moisture and tenderness of baked goods and may have the role of a preservative in some recipes. Sugar also caramelizes (browns) at high temperatures, providing textures and additional flavors. In yeast breads, sugar is necessary to feed the yeast so the dough rises. Still, in many recipes other than baked goods you can simply decrease the amount of sugar by one third without affecting the quality of the product. Substitute flour for the amount of sugar omitted. If your recipe calls for a cup of sugar, try 2/3 cup sugar and 1/3 cup flour. Many spices can be used to give the impression of sweetness without adding sugar. These include cardamom, cinnamon, nutmeg and vanilla. All are calorie free.

To increase fiber, use a whole grain (i.e., whole-wheat flour, oatmeal, or whole cornmeal) in place of white flour. Whole-wheat flour can be substituted for up to half of all-purpose flour, although whole-wheat flour is required in a lesser amount. For example, if a recipe calls for two cups of flour, substitute one cup all-purpose flour and one cup minus one tablespoon of whole-wheat flour.

Salt is a marvelous flavor enhancer and preservative but in most recipes it can be decreased or eliminated. Adding other spices and herbs can pick up the flavor if your foods are too bland. In baking, however, salt, like sugar, has other jobs to do so don't eliminate it completely.

BAKING SODA,
THE WHITE CLEANSER THAT'S GREEN

Baking soda is a great cleanser, deodorizer, and recipe ingredient. It doesn't contain harsh chemicals or detergents that can harm the environment. You can cut through grease on dirty dishes, yet it's mild enough to use for washing your hands and brushing your teeth. Here are some ways to use baking soda on outdoor trips:

Remove grease from a camp stovetop by cleaning with a solution of baking soda and white vinegar.

To remove food pieces that are burned onto a barbecue grill, place the grill in a large plastic garbage bag. Mix 1 cup baking soda with 1/2 cup ammonia, pour over the grill, close the bag and let it sit overnight. The burnt pieces will loosen, making the grill easier to clean.

Remove stubborn cooked-on food from pots and baking dishes by sprinkling with 1/2 cup baking soda and 1/2 cup white vinegar. Let the dishes soak for a few hours before cleaning.

Clean coolers with a water and baking solution to eliminate odors.

Deodorize a musty tent by setting it up and sprinkling it with baking soda. You can also deodorize sleeping bags by sprinkling baking soda inside first thing in the morning. Let the baking soda sit about six hours, then shake it out, zip open the bag, and let it sit in the sun for a few more hours.

Baking soda cleans plastic like a champ and won't scratch the surface. Just sprinkle on a sponge or rag and use as you would any cleanser.

Bonus tip for fishermen: keep fishhooks from getting rusty by sticking them in a cork or similar holder and submerging them in a box of baking soda for storage.

Camp Packing and Other Quick and Useful Ideas

Use a few corn chips (Fritos® work best) as fire starters. They are economical and efficient, and they look better in the fire than they do on your hips. Simply toss a few on the campfire or barbecue and light them with a match.

Consider pita bread instead of regular bread. Pita bread does not squash, takes up less room than standard bread, and you can fill pitas with lots of different foods, including salads.

Freeze leftover coffee or tea in cubes. Use the cubes in iced coffee or tea to keep your drink cold and to keep the flavor from becoming watered down.

Make fruit salad in a bag: Empty a can of fruit cocktail, a can of pineapple chunks (both cans not drained), a cup of coconut, a box of instant vanilla pudding, and a banana into a plastic bag and seal. Knead the bag until well mixed. Chill and serve right from the bag.

You can freeze soup stocks, leftover wines, lemon or lime juice, tomato sauce, and other liquids in ice cube trays. Put the frozen cubes in small plastic zipper bags and take with you.

Turn regular oatmeal into instant oatmeal by chopping it finer in the blender before you leave home. This also makes a healthy substitute for flour.

Evaporated canned milk and dry milk are great for camping trips. Canned milk lasts longer in the cooler than regular milk. Mix half canned milk and half water to use as a milk substitute. Powdered milk isn't popular for drinking, but it's easier to store, lighter to carry, and cheaper than regular milk, and also works nicely in recipes.

When you're buttering lots of corn on the cob, melt a stick of butter in a pan of hot water. The melted butter will float. To butter corn, simply dip the cob into the hot buttered water. The butter sticks; the water doesn't.

CHAPTER 2

HEAT SOURCES

To begin any cooking adventure you need a source of heat. Various types of portable stoves are commonly used for outdoor cooking and camping. Besides being convenient, these stoves may be the only type of appliances practical or possible in many extreme environments. In addition, many state and federal parks ban the use of campfires.

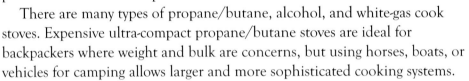

There are many types of propane/butane, alcohol, and white-gas cook stoves. Expensive ultra-compact propane/butane stoves are ideal for backpackers where weight and bulk are concerns, but using horses, boats, or vehicles for camping allows larger and more sophisticated cooking systems.

While gas stoves have their advantages, no other type of heat has the primitive complexity or alluring beauty of the campfire. The campfire's dynamic performance casts a hypnotic spell by simultaneously stimulating and entertaining all of our senses~the fire's crackling and popping sounds, its ember-laced yellow flames dancing and flowing around wood, its relaxing warm glow, and the aroma of smoke. Ever since humans "discovered" fire tens of thousands of years ago, it has been our constant companion and tool, allowing us to develop cooking and advance in nearly all aspects of life.

CAMPFIRES

Check to see if open campfires are allowed where you are going. Permanent fire restrictions may be in place in environmentally fragile areas or in place temporarily during dry spells. Some jurisdictions require special permits for fires. Build fires only in designated areas. If you are in virgin territory, build the campfire in an open area away from tall grasses, brush, and trees. When constructing a campfire, outline it with stones to form a small circle, usually no more than a couple of feet in diameter. Large fires are difficult to cook on, waste fuel, and increase the risk of initiating and spreading wildfires.

For long cooking processes, build an oblong or oval fire ring so cooking with coals can be accomplished on one end while an active fire is generating more coals at the opposite end. In this manner coals can be added to the cooking area without the obstacle of direct flames.

Rocks for fire rings should be non-porous, preferably hard, crystalline igneous rocks collected away from wet areas. Sedimentary rocks, primarily shale and siltstone, or rocks collected from stream banks and other damp areas are liable to explode and fragment upon heating. This is caused as liquid water in the rock or chemically bound water in the rock is heated to high-pressure steam.

There are dozens of ways to get a fire started and it usually begins with tinder such as wads of paper, balls of dry grasses or leaves, wood shavings, and fine twigs. These materials should be placed on the bottom with wood kindling piled on top of them, in a crossed or pyramid pattern so there is good air circulation. Windy, wet, and chilly conditions can seriously hamper attempts to ignite a fire, especially if you have damp, uncooperative tinder.

When wet weather is a possibility, take charcoal lighter fluid. Fluids are superior to solid or wax-based accelerants because the fluid readily ignites and the liquid fuel physically displaces moisture as it soaks into the wood. With a small squirt of lighter fluid on some finger-sized sticks and one match, you have instant warmth and a cooperative fire.

Once the fire is going, build it up gradually with larger sticks, eventually adding logs four- to six-inches in diameter. Except for certain cooking techniques or for light, warmth, or evening entertainment, you will want the fire to burn down to coals. There shouldn't be flames lapping at you while you are cooking.

Coals burn at very high temperatures and produce dry heat with little smoke. The yellow flames in a campfire are lower in temperature and produce smoke, which is an irritant in close quarters and can cause off flavoring of the food, especially if burning resinous woods like pine and fir. Ash, beech, birch, hickory, locust, maple, and oak make the best coals for cooking, but in many parts of the country, evergreens are the dominate trees, with occasional alternatives such as willow, aspen, or cottonwood.

While many hardwood-spoiled cooks are quick to disagree, pines and their kin will craft a fine bed of coals. It just takes a larger starting volume to make a handsome, completely charred, ash-coated bed. Make sure the pine, fir, or comparable wood is firm and dense and not spongy or falling apart.

If you can, take your own firewood. Many campsites require it to prevent depletion of the area's wood resources. By hauling your own wood you will be guaranteed wood that is high quality, dry, and clean.

WOOD CHARCOAL AND BRIQUETTES

Whether barbecuing, grilling, or baking in a Dutch oven, wood coals and briquettes are the two forms of charcoal most often used. Charcoal is the nearly pure carbon residue that remains after all or most of the organic hydrocarbons in wood have been distilled or burned off. When wood is made into charcoal, 70 to 75 percent of the wood volume is lost to evaporation and burning. Water vapor, alcohol, acetone, turpentine, and a whole host of other volatile organic compounds are formed, released, and burned during this distillation and combustion process.

Charcoal yields a greater amount of heat in proportion to its volume than a corresponding quantity of wood. Charcoal also has the advantage of being relatively smokeless while burning. Both of these qualities contribute to charcoal's desirability for cooking. Briquettes are compact, have a long burn time, and are easy to manipulate for temperature control.

Charcoal briquettes are produced by crushing lump charcoal to a powder and mixing the powder with water and binding additives, such as food starch or clay. If you're worried about additives, look carefully at different brands of charcoal briquettes. In addition to binding agents, some manufacturers dope the briquettes with nitrates and other oxidizers to enhance lighting and burning. Many manufacturers add anthracite coal to reduce costs and produce longer burning. These are usually cheap, generic brands and buying these to save a couple of dollars probably isn't worth it. While most of these additives are of little concern, anthracite coal may attach unwanted flavors and chemicals to the food. "Natural" briquettes will use only real hardwood charcoal and food starch for the binding agent.

Commercial lump charcoal is generally made from untreated hardwood lumber scraps and branches too small to mill. This charcoal is not ground or broken up and resembles the former branch or board from which it originated. Lump charcoals are pure, natural, wood charcoals and usually contain no additives.

LIGHTING THE COALS

There are several ways to light lump charcoal and briquettes, the safest being chimney stacks where charcoal is placed in a metal tower on top of some paper, which is ignited with a match. Once the charcoal is burning thoroughly, the bottom of the container is dropped away, releasing the lit charcoal into the firebox.

Lighter fluids specifically manufactured for lighting charcoal briquettes also work well. Early lighter fluids were composed of alcohol, benzene, or other highly volatile liquids which could become explosive. Lighter fluids today are produced with much lower flash points, similar to kerosene, and are odorless. Never use a flammable liquid such as gasoline that is not specifically designed for lighting charcoal.

Many people worry about lighter fluids imparting a petroleum taste to the food. If this happens it is usually because the cooking started before the charcoal briquettes were entirely gray and evenly coated with ash, or because lighter fluid was splashed onto the metal parts of the grill where it slowly evaporated into the heat column and onto the food. To avoid this, apply the lighter fluid directly on the briquettes without splashing and only use enough fuel to ignite the briquettes. A full, even coat of ash on the briquette indicates that the entire surface of the briquette is red-hot, burning carbon. Any food-tainting volatiles (such as lighter fluid) trapped within the briquette would have to pass unburned through a 2,000° reaction zone. This is not likely since lighter fluid has an ignition temperature of around 500°. Ash also acts as a catalyst for the combustion of hydrocarbons, which further decreases the probability of any intact lighter fluid molecules making it to the food.

Lump charcoal can be ignited in the same way as briquettes, but it's best to avoid lighter fluids. Lump charcoal is more porous so it absorbs the fluid more readily. It also burns more rapidly than briquettes and burns in an uneven fashion, producing hot and cool spots. Fumes from unburned lighter fluid in cool spots can contaminate the food. You can usually light lump charcoal by piling it on top of wads of crumpled paper; this will avoid any possibility of petroleum fumes tainting the food.

COOKING WITH CHARCOAL AND BRIQUETTES

Except for searing, most charcoal grills are designed to cook with the lid closed. Sear both sides of the meat with the lid open, then close the lid to prevent flare-ups and to retain the natural juices.

For large items such as roasts or whole chickens, use indirect heat by placing a pan of water on the coals directly under the food, or position the coals to one side of the grill box and place the food on the opposite side of the grill. Wine, orange juice, herbs, and spices can be tossed in the water for an extra savory flavor that will permeate the food via water vapor.

Once you've mastered lump charcoal and briquettes on a grill, you're ready to use them for other cooking methods. With a few exceptions, most of the cooking techniques in this book use charcoal as the heat source.

SMOKING FOODS WITH WOOD CHIPS

Adding soaked wood chips to the coals will imbue foods with a nice smoke flavor. The most efficient way to make smoke is to wrap water-soaked wood chips (or chunks) in aluminum foil and poke holes along the top of the sealed package. With the hole-side up, place the foil pack directly on the coals next to the water pan. The foil package keeps the aromatic flavors in the smoke from scorching in the direct heat of the coals.

GAS BARBECUES AND GRILLS

Of all outdoor cooking appliances, gas barbecues and grills score first place in convenience—that is, until you try to transport one. Due to their bulky, top-heavy design, not to mention loose parts, fuel tanks, and gas lines, most gas barbecues and grills are designed to be backyard fixtures. Many of these devices are specialized, while others have built-in rotisseries, top-plate burners, and other add-ons. Since most gas grills can be adapted for direct and indirect grilling, barbecuing, frying, smoking, baking, and other types of cooking, techniques for using gas grills are described in the cooking chapters.

CHAPTER 3

RUBS, SAUCES, AND MARINADES

There are three main categories of seasoning meats and vegetables for barbecuing: rubs (wet and dry), sauces and salsas, and marinades. These seasonings applied to food before and during the cooking process have three basic functions: flavoring, preserving or adding moisture, and enhancing the food's visual qualities. Certain fruit juices such as pineapple, other acids such as vinegar or wine, and papain or bromelain enzymes contained in many seasonings also serve as meat tenderizers.

Cooks have individual preferences about which meats and sauces to use and these differ among regions of the country. Various seasoning methods will produce different results.

WHICH SPICES TO USE

Let your taste buds be your ultimate guide; however, if you are unfamiliar with spices, the following list will get you started:

Beef: Basil, bay leaf, caraway, cayenne, chili, coriander, cumin, dill, garlic, ginger, marjoram, mint, oregano, parsley, pepper, rosemary, sage, savories, tarragon, and thyme.

Duck: Dill, hyssop, rosemary, sage, savories, and tarragon.

Fish: Allspice, anise, basil, bay leaf, caraway, cayenne, chives, coriander, curry, dill, fennel, garlic, ginger, hyssop, lemon balm, marjoram, mint, mustard, nutmeg, paprika, parsley, pepper, rosemary, sage, savories, tarragon, and thyme

Goose: Marjoram, rosemary, sage, tarragon, and savories.

Lamb: Basil, bay leaf, caraway, cardamom, coriander, cumin, curry, dill, garlic, lemon balm, hyssop, marjoram, mint, rosemary, sage, savories, thyme, and turmeric.

Liver: Coriander, sage, and tarragon.

Pork: Allspice, anise, basil, bergamot, cardamom, chervil, coriander, cloves, cumin, curry, dill, fennel, garlic, ginger, lemon balm, mint, marjoram, mustard, oregano, paprika, parsley, rosemary, sage, savory, spearmint, tarragon, and thyme.

Poultry: Allspice, anise, basil, bay leaf, caraway, coriander, cumin, dill, garlic, ginger, lemon balm, marjoram, mint, rosemary, sage, savories, tarragon, and thyme.

Shellfish: garlic, rosemary, and thyme.

DRY RUBS

The rub is the second most important part of barbecuing; the smoking technique is the first. When creating your rub there are two main concepts to keep in mind. The proportion of salt should be great enough to draw moisture from the surface of the meat through osmosis, and the proportion of sugar should not be excessive or it will caramelize and burn during smoking, leaving a bitter taste. However, since

sugar contributes to osmosis, it is important and should not be eliminated.

Your rub should be limited only by your imagination. Herbs and spices to consider include paprika, cumin, garlic powder, onion powder, black pepper, cayenne pepper, chili powder, oregano, sage, and any spice that you enjoy. Also consider seasonings such as dry mustard, cinnamon, nutmeg, and ginger to add special flavors or to nicely balance a rub mixture.

Rubs should be applied at least the night before smoking. For better flavor let the meat absorb the rub for up to three days. However, some foods, such as fish, benefit from a light application.

A shaker makes the rub mixture easy to apply. Shake the rub liberally over the entire surface of the meat. Once the rub starts to get moist and adhere to the meat, add more. It's not necessary to "rub" it in, which only results in uneven distribution and stained hands.

Once the rub is applied, wrap the meat loosely in butcher paper and leave it in the refrigerator for at least for a couple of hours before smoking.

Rubs are better than marinades for large pieces of meat such as briskets and pork butts because the internal and external fat of these large cuts will melt during the cooking process, keeping the meat moist and dispersing the rub flavor. The surface of the meat combines with rub to produce a taste-tantalizing and eye-appealing crust on the finished product.

Pastes are similar to dry rubs, differing only in that they contain an additional water or oil base. Pastes are used and applied in the same manner as dry rubs. While dry rubs collect their moisture from the meats, pastes add moisture as well as flavor. Basically a paste is a "wet" dry rub.

SAUCES

There are regional differences and preferences regarding sauces and sauce bases. Southern sauces are typically vinegar and pepper-based, although South Carolinians prefer mustard. In the Midwest and Texas, as well as farther west, the sauces are most often tomato-based and spicy. In the far West, fresh herbs and citrus fruits are commonly used. Additionally, there are Asian barbecue sauces and sauces that use alcohol such as bourbon or Zinfandel wine. There are hot sauces with chilies. However, in the commercial market, the standard tomato and ketchup-based sauces still outsell all others.

One thing almost all sauces have in common is a sweetener, either white sugar, brown sugar, honey, molasses, fruit nectars, or maple syrup. Because sugars tend to burn easily, sauces should only be used during the last hour of barbecuing and at lower temperatures. This is especially true with tomato-based sauces, which will blacken long before the meat is done.

Sauces provide an easy way change a dish from plain to "pizzazz" within a relatively short period of time. Few people have the time to prepare and simmer their own sauces, but anyone can quickly turn a commercial, store-bought product into their "own" special sauce by adding ingredients such as spinach, mushrooms, chilies, hot pepper sauces, ginger or other spices, or even fruits. Experiment by adding sweet, sour, and spicy flavors until you come up with a sauce that is right for you.

MARINADES

A marinade is a seasoned liquid that contains a tenderizing acidic ingredient such as vinegar, wine, tomatoes, soy sauce, or citrus juice. The acids soften the meat proteins. Certain juices, such as pineapple, contain bromelain and other tenderizing enzymes.

Marinades add flavor and can be made of a combination of herbs, spices, and even vegetables. They almost always contain vegetable oil, olive oil, or some other oil. The oils act as solvents to dissolve and transport spice oils and other volatile ingredients to the food. This is one reason why it is necessary to emulsify the oil and other ingredients by shaking or blending the marinade. Vegetable or olive oil may also contribute flavor.

Regardless of the ingredients, follow the recipe directions carefully since marinade times vary, depending on the food, and some foods, especially fish and shrimp, can easily become mushy if marinated too long.

Due to the acid in marinade, always marinate in a non-reactive container such as a glass or ceramic bowl or pan, or even a plastic zip-lock bag.

Marinades will penetrate foods faster at room temperatures, but if the food is to be marinated for more than one hour, let it marinate in a refrigerator or cooler. Begin marinating up to a few hours before cooking, turning the food often to ensure even distribution of the marinade.

APPROXIMATE MARINATING TIMES

Food	Hours	Food	Hours
Beef Brisket	5-8	Lamb Kabobs	4-6
Beef Kabobs	4-6	Pork Chips	3-4
Beef Short Ribs	5-8	Pork Leg	6-8
Chicken Breasts	3-4	Pork Roast	6-8
Chicken Pieces	3-4	Pork Tenderloins	3-4
Chicken Whole	4-6	Shell Fish	1/2-1
Chicken Wings	6-8	Spare Ribs	6-8
Duck	6-8	Turkey Parts	4-8
Fish	1-2	Turkey Whole	4-8
Game Birds	4-6	Venison	6-8

BASIC PORK RUB
(MAKES ABOUT 3/4 CUP)

A simple, spicy addition that puts spark in ordinary pork and it forms an eye-pleasing, crunchy, glazed crust to boot!

1/4 cup black pepper
1/4 cup paprika
3 T sugar
2 T salt
2 t dry mustard
2 t cayenne

1. Mix all ingredients.
2. Work half of the mixture onto meat 12-24 hours before cooking. Place meat in a cool place, such as a cooler or the refrigerator.
3. Apply remaining rub before barbecuing.

CARIBBEAN RUB/PASTE
(MAKES ABOUT 2 CUPS)

Very spicy and quite hot if habanero peppers are used. If you can't take the heat, substitute milder jalapeño or serrano peppers. This makes about 2 cups, which is more than you will need, so refrigerate the excess for future use.

6 T garlic, minced
6 T dried minced onion
2 T allspice
1 T dried ground chipotle pepper
2 T Hungarian paprika
2 T brown sugar
4 1/2 t minced fresh thyme
4 1/2 t cinnamon
1 1/2 t nutmeg
1/2 t ground habanero pepper
zest of 2 lemons

1. In a bowl, combine all ingredients.
2. Spread evenly on prepared meat that has been patted dry. Let sit until the rub appears moist.

CHILI RUB (MAKES ABOUT 1 1/4 CUPS)

Spicy with a little flash of heat, which makes this an interesting rub for pork and chicken. Makes about one cup, which is more than enough to cover two slabs of pork back ribs.

1/4 cup ground cumin
1/4 cup + 1 T chili powder
2 T ground coriander
1 T ground cinnamon
2 T raw sugar or brown sugar
2 T coarse, or kosher, salt
2 T coarse ground black pepper
2 T red pepper flakes

1. Place all ingredients in a jar with a tight lid or in a large zip-lock plastic bag.
2. Seal canister/bag and shake thoroughly.
3. Store at room temperature; keep covered.

CHOICE CHICKEN RUB
(MAKES ABOUT 1 1/4 CUPS)

This rub is perfect for all poultry. We use it on everything from chicken to game birds.

1/4 cup paprika
1/4 cup freshly ground black pepper
1/4 cup celery salt
1/4 cup sugar
1 T onion powder
1 T garlic powder
2 T dry yellow mustard
2 t cayenne
zest of 4 lemons, dried and minced

1. Mix all ingredients in a bowl or plastic bag.
2. Store excess in a cool dark place in a sealed jar or plastic bag.

Dearborn Rib Rub
(MAKES ABOUT 1 CUP)

A favorite from the family ranch on the Dearborn River, Montana.

1/2 cup brown sugar
1/4 cup paprika
1 T black pepper
1 T salt
1 T chili powder
3/4 T garlic powder
3/4 T onion powder
1 t cayenne

1. Mix together all ingredients and store in an airtight container.
2. Spread evenly on meats that have been patted dry. Let sit until the rub appears moist.

Garlic Rub/Paste
(MAKES ABOUT 1/2 CUP)

1/4 cup olive oil
5 cloves garlic, crushed
1 T fresh parsley
1 t cayenne

1. Mix garlic, parsley, and cayenne together.
2. Slowly add oil while mixing.
3. Refrigerate in an airtight container.

HORSERADISH RUB/PASTE

(MAKES ABOUT 2 1/2 CUPS)

3/4 cup freshly grated
    horseradish root
1/2 cup finely chopped garlic
1/4 cup kosher or canning salt
1/4 cup black pepper
1/2 cup olive oil
2 T ground cumin
1 T Dijon mustard
1 T brown sugar

1. Combine all ingredients and mix well.
2. Refrigerate in an airtight container.

ROJA COFFEE RUB

(MAKES ABOUT 1 CUP)

Excellent on all pork, but performs well on beef ribs, roasts, and game birds.
Make this rub just before use as the coffee flavor fades rapidly.

1/2 cup finely ground coffee
3 T ground ancho chili
3 T kosher or sea salt
2 T packed brown sugar
1 rounded T fresh ground black
    pepper
Add a dash of nutmeg when
    seasoning game birds
Garlic powder, to taste

1. Combine all ingredients.
2. Use immediately—rub on meat prior to
    cooking.

TROPICAL SPICE PORK RUB
(MAKES ABOUT 1 1/4 CUPS)

This rub is fabulous on pork chops or pork roasts.

2 T of each:
    ground bay leaf
    ground cloves
    ground mace
    ground nutmeg
    paprika
    thyme
1 T of each:
    ground allspice
    ground cinnamon
    ground savory
5 T white peppercorns, ground

1. Blend all spices and store in a screw-top glass jar.
2. Use approximately 1/2 t of spice rub per pound of meat.
3. Rub on meat and let sit for an hour to overnight to add an exceptionally fine flavor to pork.

WEST INDIAN RUB (MAKES ABOUT 1 CUP)

This nice rub imparts a non-traditional flavor to the barbecue.

4 T curry powder
2 T ground allspice
2 T ground cumin
3 T paprika
2 T coarsely ground black pepper
2 T coarse salt
2 T ground ginger

1. Place all ingredients in a jar with a tight lid or in a large zip-lock plastic bag.
2. Seal canister/bag and shake thoroughly.
3. Store at room temperature; keep covered until ready to use.

Chimichurri Marinade
(MAKES ABOUT 1 1/4 CUPS)

A marinade with South American zing.

6 cloves garlic
3 bay leaves
2 jalapeños, coarsely chopped, with seeds
1 1/2 T salt
1 T ancho chili powder
1/2 cup finely minced fresh cilantro
1/2 cup finely minced flat leaf parsley
1/4 cup finely minced fresh oregano leaves
1/4 cup distilled white vinegar
1/4 cup olive oil

1. In a blender, puree garlic, bay leaves, jalapeños, salt and 1 T of the vinegar until a paste is formed.
2. Transfer to a mixing bowl and add the herbs.
3. Whisk in the remaining vinegar and olive oil until smooth.
4. Add more olive oil if necessary to improve consistency.

Tarragon and Lime Supreme Chicken Marinade
(MAKES ABOUT 3/4 CUPS)

1/2 cup lime juice
1/4 cup vegetable oil
1 t tarragon
1 t onion salt
1/4 t black or white pepper

1. Combine ingredients and brush over 2 chickens cut into pieces.
2. Marinate for 3-4 hours in a cooler or refrigerator.

Ruby Basin Marinade
(MAKES ABOUT 1 1/4 CUPS)

A flavorful favorite of western Montana—excellent "all around" choice for beef, lamb, pork, or chicken.

1/4 cup red wine
1/4 cup balsamic or red wine
   vinegar
2 T olive oil
2 T soy sauce
2 T catsup
1/4 t onion salt
2 cloves garlic, minced
fresh ground black pepper to taste

1. Combine ingredients.
2. Cover meat and marinate according to approximate marinade times chart.

Tomato-Base Marinade
(MAKES ABOUT 1 3/4 CUPS)

A basic marinade that is highly prized for beef, lamb, pork, or chicken.

1 8-oz. can tomato sauce
2 T lemon juice
1 T olive oil
2 T Worcestershire sauce
1/2 T dried basil, or 1/3 cup fresh
   chopped basil leaves
1/4 t onion salt
2 cloves finely chopped garlic
black pepper to taste

1. Combine ingredients.
2. Marinate meat in a cool place (see chart on marinating times in Chapter 1).

TURKEY GINGER-BRINE MARINADE
(ENOUGH TO SUBMERGE A 20-25 LB TURKEY)

John Piquette (1946-2005) began his culinary career at age eleven, busing tables and washing dishes at Paul's Pancake Parlor in Missoula. He went on to apprentice as a baker, earned a degree from the University of Montana, and became a food service manager and culinary arts teacher. John's daughter, Colet Bartow, submitted this recipe from her father's collection. It makes enough brine to marinate a 20 lb turkey. Use a large pickle bucket or similar container. Colet marinates her turkey for up to two days. This marinade also works well for chicken pieces and pork.

2 qt apple juice or apple cider
2 lb brown sugar or 1 pt molasses
1/2 cup salt
3 pt water
3 rinds of oranges cut in julienne strips
2 T fresh ginger, diced finely
12 cloves, whole
4 bay leaves
4 cloves fresh garlic, mashed

1. Bring apple juice, sugar and salt to a boil in a large saucepan, stirring to completely dissolve sugar.
2. Cook for 1 minute and then remove from heat. Cool, and skim off any foam.
3. Add remaining ingredients. Stir well.
4. Submerge turkey and soak in cool area for 24 hours. Keep below 40° as the meat marinates.
5. Drain marinade and reserve for gravy.
6. This type of turkey is great cooked on the lowest heat setting on the barbecue grill, or on a spit. Meat should be cooked to an internal temperature of 155°.
7. To use the marinade, strain it first to remove solid pieces. Cook in an open saucepan at high heat to reduce the liquid volume by a minimum of 1/2. Used this reduced sauce as a light and tasty gravy over sliced meat.

WASABI-SOY MARINADE
(ENOUGH FOR 8-10 SERVINGS)

Here is a Japanese marinade that is especially good on shellfish.

1/4 cup water
1/4 cup soy sauce
1/4 cup Japanese mirin (sweet
   cooking rice wine)
1 scant t sugar
ginger root, medium-sized chunk,
   sliced thin
1 t wasabi paste
1 lemon, fresh, juiced
cilantro, fresh sprigs, chopped fine
black pepper, freshly ground

1. Mix all ingredients.
2. Pour over food to be marinated.
3. Let sit 30 minutes to 1 hour
   (refrigerated).

BARBECUE SAUCES

BACKYARD BARBECUE SAUCE
(MAKES ABOUT 3 CUPS)

This is a basic home barbecue sauce that will enhance just about any kind of meat. Any beer works, but the dark varieties add a richer flavor.

1/2 cup vegetable oil
1 cup chopped onions
8 cloves garlic, chopped
1 20-oz. can puréed tomatoes
1 bottle beer
2 t salt
2 T chili powder
1/4 cup cider vinegar

1. Heat a splash of the oil in a large skillet and sauté the onions until brown.
2. Reduce heat and add garlic and cook until the garlic starts to turn opaque.
3. Add tomatoes, beer, salt, chili powder, and remaining oil.
4. Bring to a boil and simmer over low heat for 20 minutes.
5. Add the vinegar and simmer for 10 minutes.

MOM'S BARBECUE SAUCE
(MAKES ABOUT 2 CUPS)

Our mother was considered one of the best cooks in the Dearborn community. When you taste her famous barbecue sauce we are sure you will agree.

14 oz. catsup
1/2 cup chili sauce
1/4 cup wine vinegar
1/4 cup brown sugar
2 T lemon juice
2 T Worcestershire sauce
2 T prepared mustard
2 T vegetable oil

2 T steak sauce
1 t dry mustard
1/4 t salt
1/4 t black pepper
1 clove garlic, minced

1. Mix ingredients in a saucepan.
2. Simmer for 30 minutes.

DIABLO BARBECUE SAUCE
(MAKES ABOUT 1 1/2 CUPS)

We highly recommend this spicier sauce for chicken and roast pork.

2 T olive oil
8 cloves garlic crushed
4 T minced onion
1 can tomato sauce
1 can tomato paste
2 T brown sugar
2 T cider vinegar
1 T Worcestershire sauce
1 t dry mustard
2 T Tabasco chipotle sauce
2 t African cayenne
fresh ground pepper to taste

1. Cook garlic and minced onion in olive oil until onions turn opaque.
2. Add remaining ingredients; mix thoroughly.
3. Simmer 20 minutes.

HONEY BARBECUE SAUCE
(MAKES ABOUT 1 CUP)

This sauce adds a sweet yet tangy flavor to most grilled foods. Honey barbecue is an excellent complement to grilled chicken, pork, and hamburgers. We tried this on salmon and it was fantastic!

1 T vegetable oil
1/4 cup onions, finely chopped
2 cloves garlic, minced
1 cup tomato sauce
1/4 cup honey
1/4 cup vinegar
2 T dry cooking sherry
1 t dry mustard
1/2 t salt
1/4 t coarse black pepper

1. Heat oil in a medium sized saucepan over medium heat.
2. Once oil is hot, add onion and garlic; stir and continue cooking until onion is soft and translucent.
3. Add remaining ingredients and bring sauce to a boil.
4. Reduce heat and simmer for 20 minutes.

CHARRED CHILE SALSA

(MAKES ABOUT 1 CUP)

1 red bell pepper
3 ripe Roma tomatoes (approx. 8 oz)
6 tomatillos, husks removed
4 garlic cloves, arranged on a wooden skewer
1/2 small white onion, peeled
1 pasilla chili (approx 1/2 oz)
1 ancho chili (approx 1/2 oz)
1 guajilla chili (approx 1/2 oz)
1 bunch fresh cilantro; reserve some sprigs for garnish
1/2 cup tomato juice
1/2 t coarse salt
2 t lime juice
2 t maple syrup or brown sugar (optional)
1 T olive oil

1. Prepare a charcoal fire with approximately 36 briquettes. When the charcoal briquettes are very hot, spread the coals into an even layer.
2. Lightly oil the skins of the red bell pepper, tomatoes, tomatillos, skewered garlic cloves and white onion half.
3. Place these vegetables over the hot charcoal fire and grill until the skins are blistered and lightly charred. Turn often. This will take about 15 minutes.
4. Remove vegetables from the fire and allow to cool. Set aside.
5. Place the chilies over the fire and lightly toast, turning frequently. This will take only 1 to 2 minutes. Take care not to burn the chilies. Remove the chilies from the fire.
6. Peel and discard the charred skins and stems and seeds of the red bell pepper; also discard the stems and seed of the toasted chilies.
7. Transfer all of the grilled vegetables to a food processor.
8. Add the remaining ingredients and process to a coarse puree. Adjust the salt and pepper to taste. If the salsa is a little too thick, add additional tomato juice or water to adjust the consistency.

HEARTY MUSHROOM SAUCE
(MAKES ABOUT 2 3/4 CUPS)

3 T butter
8 oz sliced fresh mushrooms
3 T flour
3/4 cup chicken broth
1/4 cup red wine, optional
1 T chopped chives
1 t horseradish
1/4 cup cream

1. Melt butter in medium saucepan and add mushrooms.
2. Sauté until tender.
3. Add the flour, broth, wine, chives, and horseradish.
4. Cook over medium heat, stirring constantly until thickened.
5. Stir in cream.

PICANTE SAUCE
(MAKES ABOUT 2 1/2 CUPS)

One of the most versatile sauces. Add it to a variety of dishes or use as a dip.

3 medium fresh tomatoes, seeded and diced fine
1 green bell pepper, diced fine
1/2 cup diced onion or green onions
1 Anaheim chili, diced
2 T chopped fresh cilantro
4 cloves garlic, finely chopped
2 T lime juice
1/2 t chili powder
1/2 t ground cumin
1/2 t salt

1. In medium bowl, combine ingredients; mix well. Cover. Chill.
2. Refrigerate leftovers.

RED CHILI MUSTARD
(MAKES ABOUT 2 1/4 CUPS)

This mustard can be prepared one week ahead and refrigerated. This is perfect mustard to use on beef or pork. Try it with our Grilled Rib-Eye with Chimichurri and Red Chili Mustard in Chapter 5.

2 cups Dijon mustard
3 T ancho chili powder

1. Mix mustard and chili powder together well with 3 T of lukewarm water.
2. Bring to room temperature before serving.

SWEET-HOT MUSTARD
(MAKES ABOUT 1 1/2 CUPS)

1/2 cup brown sugar, packed
1/4 cup dry mustard
1 T flour
2 eggs
1/4 cup white vinegar
1/3 cup water

1. Beat first 4 ingredients in a medium saucepan until smooth, and then stir in vinegar and water.
2. Place over medium heat and stir until thick.

CHAPTER 4

BARBECUE COOKERY

I s it barbecue or grilling? There are many interpretations of the term "barbecue." Most people use "barbecue" to describe a social gathering that involves outdoor cooking. Many people use it, incorrectly, to describe the method of "grilling" food.

The real distinction between traditional barbecue and grilling is about as plain as night and day. Grilling is cooking over a hot bed of coals or gas flames for a relatively short time. Grilling uses high temperatures, normally 500° or more, to sear meat and rapidly cook the surface of food. Since steaks, chops, and similar cuts are already tender, long cooking periods are not required. Grilling is the only way to make a steak dark brown and crisp on the outside and bloody rare on the inside.

We use the term "barbecue" to describe several types of slow-cooking techniques. The typical style of barbecue is slow cooking in continuous clouds of wood smoke with just sufficient indirect heat to cook the food. The ideal barbecue temperature is usually between 200° and 220° during the entire cooking process. Briskets, ribs, shoulders, and other tough, fibrous cuts of meat are traditional for this type of cookery where slow cooking is required to soften the collagens in the meat. In addition to tenderizing the meat, the fire in the barbecue flavors the food with a rich, deep, smoky flavor. We also include as barbecue the process of cooking in

NATIVE AMERICAN USE OF SMOKING FOODS

Before the intervention of white settlers, many Native Americans were nomadic and had adapted many methods and styles of cooking to their itinerant way of life. The Indians of the Great Plains predominantly used a smoke curing process. Strips of flesh from bison and deer were hung on sticks by the fire to slowly dry and smoke. This process doesn't reach sufficient temperatures to cook the meat, but it reduces bulk and weight by about 80 percent through dehydration, making transport and storage much more efficient. In addition to drying, the fire preserves and flavors the meat with smoke residue, which creates an excellent barrier to insects and microbial growth. The smoke-dried meat could be eaten later as is, mixed with fat and berries to make pemmican, or ground and cooked in soups.

earthen pits, which allows food to acquire a gentle, earthen-smoky flavor in contrast to the strong wood-smoke flavor typical of standard barbecue. Barbecue is slow cooking but always well worth the wait.

TRADITIONAL AMERICAN SMOKY BARBECUE

Early origins of what we call "barbecue" began with New World explorers in the West Indies. The first written record of this technique comes from Oviedo, whose Hystoria General de las Indias, or General History of the West Indies, was published in Toledo, Spain, in 1525. In his notes, Oviedo talks of the native Arawakan or Taino Indians of the Caribbean roasting animals and fish on wooden racks called "barbacoa." Paintings and illustrations from as early as 1564 show Native Americans from Florida to the Carolinas cooking meats in this manner. Still, the French claim the word "barbecue" is derived from "de barbe et queue," which loosely translates as "from beard to tail." This most likely refers to the roasting of whole goats on a spit, but it is generally not accepted by most historians as the true origin of "barbecue." European settlers rapidly adapted the Native American style of barbecue cooking to

their way of life and experimented with spices, flavorings, and sauces, as well as various barbecue techniques.

Simply put, the best way to barbecue in the traditional fashion is to start with a hardwood fire. In the early years Americans dug deep pits and filled them with logs. Once the fire burned to coals, whole carcasses were hung above the coals or cooked on ground-level grates placed over the pit. The meat was cooked through the night and into the next day with wood added as needed to sustain the coals, smoke, and low heat. This early style was modified by German immigrants, knowledgeable in the art of making sausage, to efficient brick smokehouses.

As barbecue became more popular, homemade backyard contraptions began appearing. Since a sustained, low temperature is the key to successful barbecue, these prototypes were developed with various wood-burning fireboxes offset from the barbecue chamber. Vents moved the smoke to the cooking chamber on the opposite end. These improvements, along with adjustable dampers, allowed better temperature control for slow cooking and excellent smoke circulation around the food.

Smoldering logs work best for barbecue since they produce the great volumes of dense smoke and the low even temperature required for great barbecue. Lump charcoal and briquettes have already been de-volatilized during the carbonization process, so they do not produce wood smoke. They do, however, make a good firebase for adding damp hardwood chips, chunks, or blocks on top of the coals to produce fresh smoke.

Barbecuing was the most popular form of American outdoor cooking until after World War II. The availability of choice meats, along with other socioeconomic postwar changes, catalyzed the popularity of inexpensive outdoor grills, and manufacturers produced them by the millions. Anybody who wanted a barbecue smoker had to build it themselves until the mid-1970s when a few smoker-grill combinations began to appear on the market.

Digging a pit in the ground is not always practical; however, an above-ground pit structure can be constructed with cinder blocks or rocks. A metal grate laid across the top will support the meat, which will need to be turned at least once. Ideally, a metal lid, tarp, or damp sheet can be tented over the structure to hold in the smoke and heat. Many pig roasts are done in this fashion and are so successful they have become the centerpieces of annual events. Excellent compact barbecues with separate cooking and fire chambers can be purchased for about the price of a moderate gas grill, or one can be fashioned at home if you have the tools.

Many conventional gas grills can be used to barbecue if you maintain the constant low temperature. Wood chips or pellets are the best smoke source in these grills due to the small firebox and close proximity of the food.

In a pinch, a charcoal grill can be made to work by keeping the fire to one side or by placing a drip pan filled with water below the food on the grill. The water adds moisture and prevents grease from dripping onto the coals and flaring up. This indirect grilling method, detailed in the grilling section of the next chapter, basically bridges the gap between grilling and barbecue.

As with most outdoor cookery, a high quality thermometer is an important tool that is absolutely essential to the beginner for consistent barbecue success. Windy, rainy, or cool weather can greatly reduce the temperature in the cooking environment, and these effects are not always apparent unless the cooker temperature is sampled at regular intervals and the fuel-load adjusted up or down to compensate.

WOOD TIPS

moke gives barbecue that barbecue flavor. The best choice of wood depends on the type of meat. Of course, mixing woods to create unique flavors is also fun to try. Here are some ideal woods for different meats:

ALDER: Fish, Shellfish

APPLE: Beef, Bratwurst, and Pork

CHERRY: Hamburger, Turkey, Chicken, and Lamb

HICKORY: Beef, Chicken, Fish, Pork, Ribs, Sausage, Shellfish

MAPLE: Fish, Shellfish

MESQUITE: Beef, Fish, Lamb, Poultry, Shellfish

OAK: Fish, Shellfish

PEACH: Beef, Fish, Poultry

PECAN: Beef, Chicken, Sausage.

BARBECUED BRISKET
(10 SERVINGS)

This succulent brisket is an all-time family favorite at the Blacktail Ranch.

5 lb beef brisket
2 T garlic powder
2 T onion powder
2 T black pepper
2 T cayenne
2 T paprika
1 stick of butter
1 large onion, chopped
6 cloves garlic, minced
1 cup water
7 oz beer
1/4 cup cider vinegar
2 T brown sugar
2 t Worcestershire sauce
1 t chili powder
salt
black pepper, freshly ground

1. Preheat barbecue to 210°.
2. Trim excess fat from brisket and season with garlic powder, onion powder, black pepper, cayenne, and paprika.
3. Place on rack in preheated barbecue. Prop open the lid slightly and let cook.
4. Prepare sauce: Melt butter in a saucepan and sauté onion and garlic for about 5 minutes. Add water, cider vinegar, brown sugar, Worcestershire sauce, chili powder, and a little salt and pepper to taste. Let simmer for 10-15 minutes. Add beer and stir.
5. Baste sauce over brisket about every 30 minutes.
6. Slow cook brisket for 4 to 5 hours or until done, maintaining temperature at 210°.
7. When done, remove brisket and slice thinly across the meat grain.

Texas Style Smoked Brisket
(16-20 servings)

Here is a long, slow barbecue that requires an attentive pit master. Have a good book ready. Typically a piece of meat will absorb as much smoke as it can after 8 to 10 hours, and additional smoking may impart a bitter flavor.

mesquite or fruit wood chips
8-10 lb beef brisket

1/4 cup Chili Rub (See Rub Recipes)

1. Preheat barbecue and add wood chunks or chips (if you have a commercial model follow your instruction manual).
2. Clean and dry brisket. Apply Chili Rub and let meat sit for several hours or overnight in cooler.
3. Place brisket in barbecue for 8-10 hours. Keep the smoker at about 180°.
4. To increase tenderness, remove brisket from barbecue, wrap it in aluminum foil, and place on a grill over the coals at 180-200° for a few more hours.

Barbecued Pork Spareribs
(6 servings)

A good backyard dish anytime; however if cooking in bear country, burn the bones in the campfire to avoid unwanted guests during the night.

3 lbs pork ribs
1 1/2 cups barbecue sauce (for recipes see Chapter 3, or use your favorite)

1. Using your discretion and depending upon the size of your barbecue, light about 10-15 coals. Allow barbecue to heat.
2. Clean ribs, cutting away any unwanted fat, and place in barbecue.
3. Keep the barbecue about 180-200° for a total of 6 hours. If you don't have a barbecue with a thermometer, get an oven-safe thermometer and place on the cooking surface, preferably on the side.
4. Every 2 hours, or as needed, add hardwood chunks or chips to maintain the cooking temperature and smoke.
5. After 5 hours, brush ribs liberally with heated barbecue sauce of your choice and continue cooking for another hour.

CARNE DE CHANGO (SMOKED PORK)—NOT TRADITIONAL BBQ
(4 SERVINGS)

Carne de Chango translates literally to "monkey meat." We don't anticipate you will be eating a monkey. It's just a name and in fact, you will usually see this dish listed on restaurant menus as "carne ahumada" or "smoked meat." Carne de Chango originated in the Catemaco area of Mexico. Traditionally the meat is smoked in an adobe oven, but this recipe is an easy variation that you can reproduce at home with a covered grill and wet wood chips.

2 lbs boneless pork loin
1 t kosher salt or sea salt
1 t black pepper, freshly ground
3/4 cup lime juice, fresh squeezed
10-12 garlic cloves, crushed
3-4 cups wood chips (mesquite if you prefer, or try cherry or apple for a softer
    flavor)
1 cup water
3 T Crisco shortening or vegetable oil

1. Trim pork loin of all excess surface fat and cut the loin crosswise into 3-inch sections.
2. Using a thin, sharp knife, score a shallow cut, lengthwise, along each section of meat. Open flat, then use the knife as if paring an apple and cut around each section, keeping it in one long piece about 1/4-inch thick, like a spiral.
3. Rub the meat with salt and pepper.
4. Combine lime juice and garlic in a glass or plastic dish. Add the meat, turning to dampen all areas.
5. Cover and refrigerate; marinate for 2 to 3 hours. Turn meat occasionally.
6. About a half hour before you are ready to smoke the pork, soak about 3 to 4 cups of wood chips in a quart of water. Add more water if necessary.
7. If you have a standard smoker-grill, set it up and follow directions provided. For a kettle type grill use the indirect grilling method

discussed in Chapter 5. Pile about 15 large pieces of hardwood charcoal or briquettes on one side of the grill and place a medium-sized metal container, such as a baking dish, on the other side. Set the rack about six inches above the coals. Light coals and let them burn until covered with a light coat of gray ash.

8. Add about 1 cup of the soaked wood chips to the coals. Add 1 cup water to metal container. Allow grill to warm (about 200°).
9. Meanwhile, remove pork from the marinade and pat it dry.
10. Working quickly, open grill and place the meat on the rack over the water dish. Close the lid.
11. Allow meat to continue smoking for about 40 minutes. If you have a thermometer (even a glass candy thermometer will work), watch grill carefully to keep it between 185 and 200° F. If temperature drops, add another coal to the fire. If it gets too hot, open the vents for a few minutes.
12. Occasionally add more wood chips as needed.
13. Turn the meat after about the first 20 minutes of cooking.
14. The meat will be done when it turns a light reddish color.
15. Heat oil or lard to medium high heat in a heavy saucepan or cast iron pan. Quick fry the meat strips after smoking. Fry for about 1 minute, at most, on each side. (Smoked meat strips may be kept in the refrigerator for up to a week and fried when desired.)
16. Serve strips as main meat dish with sides, or cut into small pieces to use as taco meat filling.

HICKORY-SMOKED RIBS WITH GEORGIA MOP SAUCE (6-8 SERVINGS)

The South is famous for grilled ribs. There are many good southern rib recipes, but this one is by far a favorite.

3 handfuls hickory wood chips
3 slabs baby back pork ribs,
    3 1/2 to 4 lbs
1 1/2 cups beer or water
1/4 cup vegetable oil
1 yellow onion, minced
2 cloves garlic, minced
2 cups tomato puree

1/4 cup ketchup
1/4 cup cider vinegar
1/4 cup orange juice
1/4 cup firmly packed dark brown sugar
2 T Dijon mustard
1 T Worcestershire sauce
Salt and freshly ground pepper, to taste

1. Prepare a medium hot fire for indirect heat cooking in a covered grill according to manufacturer's instructions. Position rack 4-6 inches from fire.
2. Soak 3 handfuls of hickory chips in water to cover for at least 20 minutes.
3. Place each rib slab on a piece of heavy-duty aluminum foil. Sprinkle with 3 to 4 tablespoons of beer or water.
4. Wrap tightly and place on grill rack.
5. Cover grill, open vents, and cook, 45-50 minutes.
6. Prepare sauce: Over medium heat, warm oil, add onion and garlic, and sauté until tender, about 5 minutes. Stir in tomato puree, ketchup, vinegar, orange juice, brown sugar, mustard, Worcestershire, salt and pepper. Bring to a boil, reduce heat to low, and cook until thick, about 15 minutes.
7. Sprinkle soaked hickory chips over hot coals.
8. Remove foil from ribs, return to grill rack, and cover grill, partially closing the vents.
9. Grill, turning occasionally, until tender, 20-25 minutes.
10. During last 10 minutes of grilling, brush ribs with sauce.

SOUTHERN PULLED PORK SHOULDER (10-12 SERVINGS)

This recipe is worth the effort and the wait. It uses the hybrid indirect grilling barbecue technique. For the best results, start this recipe the night before to allow rub to sink in, and plan for five to six hours of cooking time. You can barbecue the shoulder in the traditional fashion as well, but plan on an extra two to three hours of cooking time with the lower temperature.

5-6 lb boneless pork shoulder, tied
Rustic Rub
Hardwood chips
1 1/2 cups cider vinegar
1/2 cup bourbon or whiskey
2 T molasses

1 1/2 cups water
2 chipotle peppers, chopped
2 T coarse salt
2 T coarse ground fresh black pepper
2 t cayenne pepper

1. Prepare Rustic Rub (see rub recipes in Chapter 3).
2. Rub all surfaces of pork shoulder with Rustic Rub; cover and refrigerate up to 24 hours in advance.
3. Soak hardwood chips in water for about 1 hour.
4. Prepare smoker (a covered grill with banked coals works as well) and heat to a medium heat.
5. Place pork shoulder on grill rack and add soaked hardwood chips to coals. Continue to add chips and charcoal to maintain heat at 250-300°.
6. Prepare basting sauce by mixing remaining ingredients. You will use the basting sauce during the last 2 hours of cooking.
7. Cooking time is approximately 5 to 6 hours. Cook to an internal temperature of 180°, basting every 20-30 minutes during the last two hours of smoking.
8. Boil leftover basting sauce for a minimum of 5 minutes.
9. When the pork shoulder is done, place it on a sturdy surface and cut into the shoulder. Using a large fork, pull the meat from the roast to make "shreds."
10. Serve with heated basting sauce. Great as sandwiches; can also be rolled in tortillas or large green lettuce leaves for a low-carbohydrate diet.

SMOKED SALMON FILLETS
(6 SERVINGS)

This recipe is an excellent example of how you can use your charcoal grill with soaked wood chips to add a smoky flavor. Start this recipe the night before, because the salmon needs time to soak in the brine. Since the heat on individual grills tends to vary, cooking time for this recipe will be from 30 minutes to an hour. It is important to regulate the heat so that the wood chips will smoke and the briquettes will burn but not flame. When the salmon is done, it will feel firm and have a nice glazed coating.

1 qt water
1 cup brown sugar, packed
1 cup white granulated sugar
1/4 cup sea salt
6 salmon filets (5-6 oz each) with skin
3+ cups alder wood chips, soaked

1. Stir water, sugars and salt in a large bowl until the sugar and salt dissolve.
2. Add salmon, skin side up, to this sugar brine and press to submerge it.
3. Cover and let sit in refrigerator overnight.
4. Remove salmon from brine and discard brine.
5. Rinse salmon under cold water and place on a baking rack, skin side down. Place in refrigerator and allow to dry, do not pat dry. You may want to put foil or a cookie sheet under the rack to catch any drippings while in the refrigerator. This will take about an hour. You want the salmon to feel dry to the touch.
6. Soak alder wood chips in water for 30 minutes.
7. Prepare grill for medium low heat.
8. Use two layers of aluminum foil and make a 12 x 10 inch rectangle with 1-inch raised sides.
9. Place 3 cups of the alder wood chips onto the foil rectangle.
10. Poke holes in the foil and set the foil pack on top of the coals for 5 minutes before grilling salmon.

11. Position your grill rack at least six inches above briquettes and wood chips. Set the vents to control the heat so that the chips smoke and the coals burn but do not flame.
12. Using three layers of foil, make another foil rectangle as before. This time, pierce six holes in the foil using a skewer, evenly spacing them over the bottom of the rectangle.
13. Arrange salmon on foil, skin side down.
14. Place salmon and foil on grill.
15. Cover grill and cook until salmon is firm to touch and a glaze has formed (30 minutes to 1 hour depending on grill heat).
16. Add more alder chips to the coals if necessary.
17. Remove salmon from foil, leaving skin on foil.
18. Transfer salmon to plate and serve hot or at room temperature.

CHAPTER 5

GRILL COOKERY

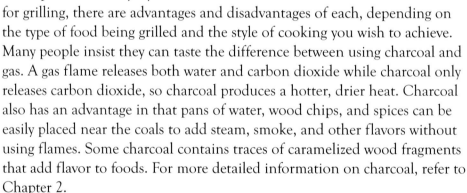

G rilling is by far the most popular form of outdoor cooking. It grew in popularity in the U.S. during the 1940s and 1950s and has become a worldwide trend.

Many styles of charcoal, gas, and electric grills have been developed. While any style works well for grilling, there are advantages and disadvantages of each, depending on the type of food being grilled and the style of cooking you wish to achieve. Many people insist they can taste the difference between using charcoal and gas. A gas flame releases both water and carbon dioxide while charcoal only releases carbon dioxide, so charcoal produces a hotter, drier heat. Charcoal also has an advantage in that pans of water, wood chips, and spices can be easily placed near the coals to add steam, smoke, and other flavors without using flames. Some charcoal contains traces of caramelized wood fragments that add flavor to foods. For more detailed information on charcoal, refer to Chapter 2.

The grills we use are mostly simple metal grates supported on rocks over a bed of coals (our "grills for the hills") and the portable, stand-up "kettle-style" charcoal grills. Sometimes we use the more sophisticated propane gas grills for backyard applications.

The key to any successful grilling is controlling the heat. Heat control with gas grills is achieved by simply raising and lowering the flames. Charcoal grills require moving coals in the firebox and keeping a certain number of coals burning at any time. Grills over campfires can be adjusted by manipulating the coals in the fire pit and, unlike kettle-style grills, there are no limitations on the height that grills can be placed in the heat column. (Just add or remove the supporting rocks.) Any type of grill will work for recipes that call for direct heat, indirect heat, or smoking.

Direct heat is used for searing and cooking small items that cook rapidly or don't require complete cooking all the way through, such as steaks, kabobs, and some vegetables. Direct heat is the only way to cook a steak that is brown and crispy on the outside and still red in the middle. Sauces and marinades will char rapidly in intense, direct heat, especially if they contain sugars, so care must be used when cooking with these seasonings. Direct heat cooking is also subject to flare-ups from dripping fats so keep a spray bottle of water handy to quench the flames. Adding pre-soaked wood chips directly to the coals or flames of a hot fire can give food a more pungent, acrid, smoky flavor since most of the light, mild-flavored aromatics will burn up in the intense heat before they can evaporate into the smoke column.

Indirect heat is a slow-cooking grilling technique that uses reflected, moderate heat at temperatures of around 200° to 300°. This method is used for cooking larger pieces of food like roasts, or vegetables like potatoes or squash that take longer to cook. Poultry, pork, and other foods that need to be thoroughly cooked should always be cooked with indirect heat. Some foods like roasts or bone-in chicken call for first searing at high heat and then roasting at low heat. This can be achieved on a gas grill by adjusting the flames. With charcoal, adjust the coal thickness to create high and low heat zones across the grill.

Many gas grills have box bottoms specifically designed to line with chunks of pumice ("lava rocks") or "briquettes and coals" made of porous, inert ceramics. These faux charcoals serve two main functions. They conduct heat from the gas flames and release it back as radiant heat in an even manner across the firebox much like real charcoal, and they capture drippings and vaporize them back into the heat column to produce the "charcoal flavor" as with real charcoal. In recipes for indirect grilling we will simply include pumice rocks and ceramic materials as "coals" since they function in the same capacity.

Adding damp spices or pre-soaked wood chips to the coals for flavoring or "smoking" is best done using indirect heat. Add these materials to a pan placed alongside the coals, or better yet, fold them into a pouch of aluminum foil, poke holes along the top of the pouch, and place it next to the coals. You don't want these flavorings to burn by placing them directly on the coals or flames because their delicate flavors will be destroyed; you want them to slowly smolder and gently evaporate into the heat column and onto the food.

PREPARING FOOD FOR THE GRILL

Grilling is an art that requires skills in both seasoning the food and being able to tell when it is perfectly done. Seasoning is best if completed before the food is placed on the grill. Salt, pepper, herbs, rubs, and sauces applied before grilling add flavor while contributing to the formation of a savory, caramelized crust that seals in juices and keep foods tender. While salt and sugar draw moisture out of meat due to osmotic differentials, this is not important unless the meat is left to sit for long periods before cooking. Unless you're using fatty cuts of meat or marinades containing oil, foods should be lightly brushed or sprayed with vegetable oil before grilling. This helps keep fragile foods like fish from sticking to the grill and helps seal in moisture, and the oil absorbs and distributes smoky flavors into the food.

PREPARING THE GRILL

Make sure the grill is clean and free of charred grease and burned food debris. It works best to remove residue from the grill with a steel brush while the grill is still warm. Clean the grill with a wire brush or wadded ball of aluminum foil after each use to prevent accumulations of food debris. To kill any residual bacteria, make sure the grill is hot before you start cooking, lightly oiling the grill with vegetable oil or cooking oil sprays will help keep foods from sticking and help protect the grill from rusting.

TIP FOR MAKING A NON-STICK GRILL

To keep delicate meats like fish or seafood from sticking to the grill, slice a raw potato in half lengthwise. Once the grill is hot, slide the cut potato down the grill in one direction only. It should make a loud hissing noise. The starch from the potato will coat the grill and act as an anti-sticking agent.

SEAFOOD ON THE GRILL

Seafood is a natural candidate for outdoor cooking. Salmon, halibut, pollock, cod, sole, or shellfish—it's not only delicious but healthy and takes little time to prepare.

To start a grill fire for seafood, use lump charcoal or briquettes, applying the methods and procedures described in Chapter 2. Fish cooks best over a medium-hot fire. Shellfish requires a hot fire. The proper temperature can be determined by holding your hand about three inches above the grill. If you must move your hand away after about two seconds, you have a medium-hot fire.

For a smokier flavor, cover the grill during cooking. Adding water-soaked hardwood chips or spices to the fire will give subtle flavor variations.

If you're using a gas grill, try to provide a smooth, even source of heat. A gas grill doesn't get as hot as a wood or charcoal fire, so it is safe to use the highest heat setting. Preheat the grill for about 10 minutes before you start cooking.

Cut the fish into individual steaks or fillets. Fillets cook faster and are easier to handle than whole fish. Oil the fish lightly on both sides just before placing it on the grill. If you are grilling a large piece of fish, you may want to wrap it in a strip of bacon to help hold the fish together. The melting fat of the bacon will baste the fish, keeping it from drying out, while adding a smoky flavor. Because seafood is delicate, turn it only once during the cooking process.

Begin by placing fish skin-side up on the grill. If the skin has been removed, the skin side will appear slightly darker. By cooking this way, the natural fat beneath the skin will be drawn down into the fillet, keeping it rich and moist. When turned, the meat side will then be face up, making an easy transition to a platter for an appealing presentation. To turn fish on the grill, use a large two-prong kitchen fork and a metal spatula. Insert the fork between the grill bars and lift the fish slightly, then slide the metal spatula under the fish and turn.

Avoid overcooking. Seafood cooks rapidly and will continue to cook a bit more after it's removed from the heat. A good rule of thumb is to cook fish 6 to 12 minutes per inch of thickness. Seafood changes from translucent to opaque as it cooks; remove fish when it is opaque throughout. You should be able to easily lift out the central bone when the fish is fully cooked.

There are a wide variety of herbs and seasonings that go well on fish. Fish of all kinds tastes great when basted with Italian salad dressing, white vermouth, lemon juice, or a mixture of mayonnaise, garlic, and your other favorite seasonings.

GRILLING SHELLFISH

Many folks cook crustaceans such as shrimp and even lobster on the grill; however, few people realize that you can grill other types of shellfish. Grilling mollusks (oysters, clams, and mussels) involves steaming. Their shells act as miniature pans and the heat causes them to steam in their own juices. Mollusks have built-in "timers"—when fresh their shells are tightly closed but they pop open when they are finished cooking. Any shell that doesn't open

should be discarded. Scallops are an exception to the closed-shell rule. If purchased in their shells, scallops are still alive (as are clams and mussels) and their shells will be slightly open. Watch them carefully during cooking to see when the shells open fully, indicating they are done. Prepare a sauce of your choice in a baking pan on the grill and add the shellfish to the pan as soon as they have finished cooking. The juices from the mollusks will mix with the sauce, infusing it with flavor. You can serve your guests directly from this pan. Toast some bread on the grill to serve with these succulent morsels and you have an easy, appetizing first course.

GRILLING VEGETABLES

Grilling vegetables is straightforward. The general rule is to cut vegetables into pieces that will cook quickly and evenly. All pieces should be the same size and no more than about 3/4 to one inch in thickness. Soak vegetables in cold water for about 30 minutes before grilling to keep them from drying out. Pat dry, then brush lightly with oil to prevent sticking.
Cook vegetables on low to medium heat to prevent scorching the tender edges. Avoid overcooking them and you will have vegetables better than you thought possible. If you like grilling vegetables and want to try smaller vegetables or cuts, use a grilling basket to keep the pieces out of the fire. Apply the same technique with fruits.

GRILL RECIPES

Cooking times are given as guides only. The times will vary depending on the type of food, grill, fire, and ambient conditions.

BURGUNDY BEEF KABOBS
(4-6 SERVINGS)

Take a taste trip to Argentina with this wonderful kabob recipe. Traditionally the food would be skewered on Burgundy grape vines soaked in water. Use them if you can find them; otherwise, standard skewers are fine.

16 wood skewers, soaked in water for 1 hour
4 lbs beef sirloin, cut into 2-inch cubes
1 cup Burgundy wine
1/4 cup and 2 T olive oil, divided
4 cloves garlic, chopped
2 shallots, diced
2 T chopped fresh rosemary
2 T green peppercorns in brine, drained and crushed
2 T Dijon mustard
1 T juniper berries
2 medium zucchini
2 red bell peppers, halved, seeded
2 yellow bell peppers, halved, seeded
2 medium red onions, peeled
24 crimini or shiitake mushrooms, washed
1/4 cup balsamic vinegar
kosher salt and freshly ground pepper

1. In large bowl prepare marinade by combining wine, 1/4 cup olive oil, garlic, shallots, rosemary, peppercorns, mustard, and juniper berries. Mix well.
2. Add beef cubes, tossing to coat well.
3. Cover with plastic wrap or lid. Refrigerate for 4 to 6 hours.
4. After marinating, thread beef onto 8 skewers. Set aside. Reserve marinade.
5. Preheat grill to high.
6. Cut zucchini, red and yellow peppers, and onions into large pieces. Thread vegetables onto remaining 8 skewers, alternating each with a mushroom.
7. In a glass bowl, combine remaining 2 tablespoons olive oil with the vinegar. Brush vegetables with this mixture. Season to taste with salt and pepper.
8. Grill beef skewers for 2 to 3 minutes per side (8 to 10 minutes total cooking time for medium-rare), basting frequently with marinade.
9. When beef has been cooking for 3 minutes, place the vegetable skewers on the grill and cook for 6 to 8 minutes until tender, brushing with remaining oil and vinegar mixture.
10. Remove all skewers from grill and serve.

GRILLED RIB-EYE WITH CHIMICHURRI MARINADE AND RED CHILE MUSTARD

(ONE STEAK PER PERSON)

This recipe is sure to impress guests. We recommend serving these steaks with a big green salad and a bottle of fine Cabernet or Beaujolais. The marinade and mustard recipes can be found in Chapter 3.

10-ounce rib-eye steaks, 1 per person
Chimichurri Marinade
1 1/2 cups Red Chili Mustard

1. Prepare Chimichurri Marinade—make enough to cover and soak all steaks in a glass pan or plastic zipper bag.
2. Cover rib-eye steaks with marinade and let marinate for 4 hours.
3. Prepare Red Chili Mustard.
4. Prepare a wood or charcoal grill and let it burn to embers.
5. Remove steaks from marinade and grill steaks until done to your liking, about 4 minutes on each side for medium rare.
6. Serve with Red Chili Mustard to taste.

CAJUN RIBS (4 SERVINGS)

When cooking ribs on the grill, wrap the ends of the ribs in foil to prevent charring the bone.

4 lbs spare ribs
3 T chili powder
3 t black pepper
2 t salt
2 t onion powder
2 t garlic powder
1 t thyme
1 t oregano

1. Mix dry ingredients.
2. Trim and clean ribs. Rub ribs with spices and let sit for 1 hour, refrigerated.
3. Preheat grill.
4. Cook ribs over indirect heat for about 45 minutes. Turn once. Watch carefully to avoid burning.
5. The ribs are done when a knife passes easily into the meat between the ribs and you can see no pink.

GRILLED PORK TENDERLOIN (4-6 SERVINGS)

These pork tenderloins have an oriental flare. Serve with rice and steamed vegetables for a tasty, healthy meal.

2 lbs pork tenderloin
1/2 cup soy sauce
1/2 cup white wine
4 green onions, chopped

3 cloves garlic, minced
1/2 t ground black pepper
1 T fresh ginger, grated

1. Mix together soy sauce, wine, onions, garlic, pepper, and ginger.
2. Place tenderloin in a flat baking dish and pour marinade over top. Let sit overnight in a cooler or refrigerator.
3. Preheat grill.
4. Grill tenderloin over medium flame, reserving marinade.
5. Grill until the internal temperature reaches 160°.
6. While the tenderloin is grilling, strain marinade and boil on high heat for 5 minutes.
7. When the tenderloin is done, remove from grill and drizzle with cooked marinade.

GRILLED LAMB WITH GARLIC AND ROSEMARY (8 SERVINGS)

4 lbs boneless sirloin lamb steaks
2 T chopped fresh garlic
2 T chopped fresh rosemary
1/2 cup good dry red wine (Merlot or Cotes-du-Rhone)
1/2 cup olive oil
salt and freshly ground black pepper to taste

1. Chop the garlic and rosemary together to form a paste. Rub the steaks with the paste and place in a glass or stainless (non-corrosive) shallow bowl.
2. Pour the wine and olive oil over the meat and cover. Marinate in the refrigerator or cooler at least 4 hours.
3. Light the grill and let it burn down until it's medium hot (not raging hot!). Sprinkle the steaks with the salt and pepper and grill (watch carefully, the fat tends to catch fire) 6-8 minutes per side for medium-rare.
4. Let the meat rest for 5 minutes before slicing.

GRILLED SESAME CHICKEN SKEWERS (4 SERVINGS)

1/4 cup coriander seeds
2 T white peppercorns
1/4 cup sesame seeds
2 1/2 t soy sauce
1 1/2 t fresh lime juice
1 T dark brown sugar
1 T liquid hot pepper seasoning
2 lbs chicken breast, boneless, skinless, cut into large chunks
4 green onions, chopped fine
2 T ginger, minced
2 T sesame oil
2 red bell peppers, halved, seeded and quartered
2 red onions, peeled, quartered
salt and freshly cracked black pepper, to taste
2 limes, quartered, for garnish

1. Prepare shake topping:

   In a small sauté pan, combine the coriander, peppercorns, and sesame seeds and toast over medium heat, shaking the pan, until the first wisp of smoke appears, 2 to 3 minutes.

   Remove from the heat and allow shake to cool.

   Place the toasted spices on a flat surface and place a small sauté pan on top of them. Holding the handle with one hand, place the other hand palm side down in the center of the pan and apply pressure, rolling the pan over the spices to crack them.

2. Make the dipping sauce:

   In a small bowl, combine the soy sauce, lime juice, brown sugar, and liquid hot pepper seasoning. Mix well, and set aside.

   In a medium bowl, combine the chicken chunks, green onions, ginger, and sesame oil and toss well.

3. Thread the chicken onto skewers alternately with the bell pepper and onion chunks, sprinkle with salt and pepper to taste, and grill over a medium fire 5-7 minutes per side. To check for doneness, cut into one of the pieces of chicken. It is done when it is opaque all the way through.

4. Place the chicken skewers on a platter, sprinkle with the shake topping, garnish with the lime wedges, and serve with the dipping sauce on the side.

FISH AND SEAFOOD

Add lemon peels to coals when grilling seafood dishes. Whole, unpeeled fresh bulbs of garlic can also be placed in the coals to add aroma and subtle flavor to many grilled dishes.

GRILLED MAHI-MAHI WITH MANGO AND BLACK BEAN SALSA
(6 SERVINGS)

6 mahi-mahi fillets (about 7 oz each) salt and freshly ground black pepper
2 t olive oil Mango and Black Bean Salsa

1. Make salsa at least 30 minutes in advance.
2. Prepare an outdoor grill.
3. Coat the fish with the olive oil and season with salt and pepper.
4. Grill fillets about seven-eight inches from the heat source for 1 1/2 minutes. Rotate the fillets 45 degrees to make an attractive crosshatch pattern and cook 1 1/2 minutes more.
5. Turn over and cook for another 1 1/2 minutes. The fish is done when it is almost firm.
6. Remove the fillets to plates, crosshatched side up.
7. Stir the salsa, spoon it generously over the fish, and serve.

MANGO AND BLACK BEAN SALSA
(6 SERVINGS)

1 14-16 oz can black beans 1/4 tsp red pepper flakes
1 mango chopped 1/4 cup freshly chopped cilantro
1/2 cup pineapple, chopped 3 tsp fresh lime juice
small onion, minced
1 garlic clove, minced

Toss all ingredients together until mixed.

Grilled Citrus Salmon
(2 servings)

2 salmon steaks or fillets
1 T olive oil
2 cloves minced garlic
1/2 cup orange juice concentrate
juice of 1/2 lemon
juice of 1/2 lime

1. Sauté garlic in olive oil.
2. Add orange juice concentrate, lemon and lime juice, and stir until heated.
3. Remove from heat and add all other ingredients.
4. Marinate fish in sauce for 1 hour, then grill or broil, basting with sauce.
5. Place on grill approximately 6-12 minutes per side depending on thickness.

Grilled Shellfish (4-8 servings)

Butter and herbs can be added directly to the morsels for maximum flavor. This serves four as a light main course, or up to eight as an appetizer.

48 assorted shellfish, such as mussels, clams, oysters, scallops, scrubbed and de-bearded
1/2 pound (2 sticks) unsalted butter
1/2 cup freshly squeezed lemon juice

1/2 cup dry white wine
3 cloves minced garlic
1 T crushed red pepper
salt and pepper to taste
4 thick slices French bread
3/4 cup fresh flat-leaf parsley, chopped

1. Heat charcoal grill until coals are white-hot, 30 to 40 minutes.
2. Place baking pan on grill; add butter, lemon juice, wine, garlic, red pepper, salt, and pepper.
3. As butter melts, arrange shellfish in a single layer on the grill.
4. Cook until shells pop open, 2 to 5 minutes; meanwhile, toast bread on edge of grill.
5. Transfer opened shells to pan of sauce; sprinkle with parsley; discard unopened shells. Serve immediately with bread.

GRILLED RAINBOW TROUT
(8 SERVINGS)

If you like to fish, this is the ultimate justification.

8 rainbow trout, cleaned
2 eggs
2 T half and half
3 cloves garlic, finely chopped
1 t dried parsley
1/2 t allspice
8 strips broiled bacon

1. Beat eggs and blend with half-and-half, garlic, and spices.
2. Dip the fish in mixture, coating the fish inside and out. Place broiled bacon in the cavity of each fish.
3. Place fish on lightly oiled grill 4-6 inches above coals.
4. Cook for 15 minutes, turning once.

GRILLED RED SNAPPER
(8 SERVINGS)

The traditional Mexican way to cook fish is to place it on a banana leaf. If you can find them, wash the leaf and place the wet leaf on the grill. Then add the fish. This works well to keep the fish from sticking to the grill and to keep it from falling apart when you turn it.

1 whole red snapper, split and
   butterflied (about 2 lbs worth)
1/2 cup achiote paste
1/2 cup orange juice
3 T lemon juice
3 T lime juice

1. Mix achiote paste (you should be able to find it in a Mexican market) with citrus juices. Coat the entire fish with this mixture.
2. Place fish in refrigerator or cooler and let sit for at least 2 hours.
3. Light grill and heat to a medium temperature.
4. Oil grill and place fish skin side up. When fish is about halfway done (about 5 minutes), turn and continue cooking another 3 minutes.
5. Top with a heated salsa.

Shrimp Grilled in Cornhusks with Charred Chile Salsa
(4 servings)

This recipe looks a bit complicated but it's really not, and it's worth the effort! The cornhusks form a steam jacket that retains the succulence of the shrimp while adding a subtle corn flavor.

1 red onion, peeled and cut into quarters or wedges
1 T olive oil
8 jumbo shrimp, peeled, tails intact

4 dried or fresh cornhusks, soaked in water
1 ripe avocado, peel and cut into 8 slices
fresh cilantro sprigs
1 lime, cut into wedges

1. If you are planning to take this meal away from home, first prepare Charred Chile Salsa (Chapter 3) and gather other ingredients for the cooler at home.
2. Prepare a charcoal fire with approximately 36 briquettes. When the charcoal briquettes are very hot, spread the coals into an even layer.
3. Brush red onion slices with olive oil. Lightly salt and pepper. Grill the slices until nicely browned, set aside.
4. Tie the cornhusks at one end with a piece of string or strip of cornhusk (like tamales). Divide the grilled red onions between the cornhusks.
5. Spoon 1-2 T of Charred Chile Salsa over the onions in each husk.
6. Place 2 shrimp in each cornhusk on top of the salsa and onions.
7. Add a few more charcoal briquettes (8-10) to the charcoal fire if the coals have died down. The fire does not have to be very hot.
8. When the fire is ready, place the shrimp-filled cornhusks on the grill. Close the lid and grill for approximately 15-20 minutes (depending on the heat of the fire) or until cooked.
9. Remove the cornhusks from the grill.
10. Place 2 slices of ripe avocado and some cilantro sprigs over the shrimp in each cornhusk.
11. Transfer the cornhusks to dinner plates and garnish with a lime wedge.
12. Drizzle a small amount of olive oil over each dish.
13. Serve with the additional salsa on the side.

GRILLED ARTICHOKES (8 SERVINGS)

1 lemon
8 small artichokes trimmed and halved
3 cloves garlic
3 sprigs thyme
2 T olive oil, plus more for brushing
salt to taste

1. Preheat grill to low-medium heat.
2. Cut lemon in half and squeeze the juice from one half into a bowl. Save for later.
3. Cut remaining half of lemon into quarters.
3. Boil artichokes in water with 2 teaspoons olive oil, garlic, lemon quarters and thyme. Cook until artichokes are just tender, approximately 35-45 minutes.
4. Remove from water, set aside and allow to dry about 5 minutes. Brush with more olive oil and place on grill.
5. Grill for about 3 minutes or until they start to brown. Sprinkle with lemon juice and salt.

GRILLED ASPARAGUS (4 SERVINGS)

1 lb fresh asparagus spears
olive oil
sesame oil

1. Cut ends off asparagus, leaving tips.
2. Soak in water for 30 minutes to an hour.
3. Pat dry and brush with olive oil and a dab of sesame oil.
4. Place on grill, turning every minute. Remove when tips start to brown.

GRILLED CORN ON THE COB
(1-2 SERVINGS PER COB)

Outstanding! The shucks protect the corn from the intense heat, keeping the kernels moist and tender while the corn cooks in its own steam. Buy corn on the cob with shucks intact. For a delicious variation, try rubbing fresh lime wedges on the cooked corn and sprinkling it with red pepper instead of the standard butter, salt, and pepper.

fresh sweet corn on the cob in husks
butter
salt and pepper to taste

1. Gently pull back the husks but don't remove from stalk.
2. Remove the silks and cut off the tip of the corn.
3. Re-wrap the husks over the ears of corn.
4. Place corn with the shucks on in cold water and soak for 1 hour.
5. Place corn, shucks and all, on a hot grill 6-8 inches from the coals and grill for 30-40 minutes.
6. Rotate periodically during grilling.
7. Serve with softened butter, salt and pepper.

SQUASH KEBOBS (6 SERVINGS)

These make a fun side dish. The key is to make sure the squash is cooked all the way through without over-browning. Cook over indirect heat with the grill cover closed to avoid burning.

6 bamboo skewers
1 1/2 lbs winter squash
1/2 cup melted butter, divided
2 T honey or brown sugar
salt and pepper to taste

1. Soak bamboo skewers in water for at least 30 minutes.
2. Peel squash, remove seeds, and cut into two-inch cubes.
3. Preheat grill with a hot fire. If using a charcoal grill, prepare it for indirect grilling. If using a gas grill, turn off burners on one side.
4. Thread squash onto skewers and brush with 1/4 cup of the melted butter.
5. Place skewers on the unheated side and cook with the lid down for 15-20 minutes.
6. While the squash is grilling, mix remaining melted butter with honey (or brown sugar).
7. When the squash is done, remove from skewers and toss with butter mixture. (The squash is done when it is soft enough to be easily pierced with a fork.)
8. Serve hot.

GRILLED PEARS (4 SERVINGS)

Pears can be cooked on the top rack of a two-tiered grill or left on the cooling grill while you eat the main course. They have a slightly sweet flavor and are especially delicious with a scoop of vanilla ice cream.

2 large ripe pears
1 cinnamon stick (about 2 inches)
$1/2$ cup white wine
1 T sugar
$1/2$ t nutmeg

1. Spray a grill-safe baking dish with cooking spray.
2. Cut pears in half from the top and remove seeds.
3. Place pears face down in baking dish and place a cinnamon stick in the center of the pan, between the pears.
4. Add wine to the dish and sprinkle sugar and nutmeg over pears.
5. Cover with aluminum foil and place on preheated grill for about 15 minutes.
6. Remove when most the liquid is gone and pears are easily pierced with a fork.

APACHE BREAD (1 LOAF)

Apache Bread is an example of ancient American Indian fare. This recipe was passed down to our grandmother Minnie from several generations before her.

1 cup yellow corn meal
1 cup white corn meal
1 t salt
1/2 t cayenne
1/2 cup bacon drippings
1 cup boiling water
Cornhusks

1. Sift corn meals with salt and red pepper.
2. Add bacon drippings and water, and beat.
3. Form in oblong shapes and wrap with cornhusks.
4. Tie with string and bake in closed grill at 350° (medium heat) for 1 hour.

DEEP-PIT BARBECUE

D eep-pit barbecue is an ideal cooking method for campers who want to spend the day afield and then come back to a ready-to-eat hot meal. Pioneer cookbooks often described this method for preparing several hundred pounds of meat. Cowboy crews used it "cuz it's easy on the cook." Modern events sometimes feature backhoe-excavated pits big enough to feed large groups of people. We include this cowboy-style barbecue not only because it's easy, but because it's so damned good.

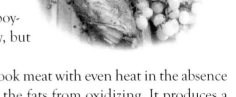

The idea of pit barbecue is to slowly cook meat with even heat in the absence of air. The lack of oxygen helps protect the fats from oxidizing. It produces a tender texture and a unique, smoky-earthen flavor that you'll never forget.

Cooking in shallow earthen pits is common among many cultures, but the depth of this pit along with its tight earthen seal makes it unique and interesting. Properly constructed, these pits can be left unattended without the danger of a fire spreading or the food burning.

GETTING STARTED

Since you may want to try this method on a small scale before inviting 200 guests over, these instructions are suited for a large family or small group of people.

YOU WILL NEED:

shovel or spade
rake
burlap feed bags
heavy-duty aluminum foil or sheet metal
roll of wire
pliers
large supply of dry firewood
smooth rocks to line fire pit
bucket of water

MAKING THE PIT

To roast 10-25 pounds of meat, dig a hole three feet deep and at least three feet wide and three feet long. Dig the pit in a dry area away from trees or buried utility lines, and avoid gravelly soils or wet areas. (The length of the pit depends on the amount of meat to be cooked at one time. For 200 to 300 pounds of beef, the pit needs to be four feet deep and at least six feet long.) Line the bottom of the pit with a layer of smooth rocks. The rocks absorb and hold heat more efficiently than soil, especially if the soil is damp, so fewer coals are required. Start a wood fire in the pit three hours or more before you add the meat, so be sure to have plenty of firewood. Use hardwood logs like hickory or oak if you have them, or fruitwoods like apple, cherry, and peach. If softwoods are all you have, start with about 30 percent more wood to make the same amount of coals. Never use treated posts or painted wood for any kind of cooking. Keep adding wood until the fire produces a bed of coals at least one foot thick. You don't have to worry about having too many coals, but not having enough can be a cooking disaster.

You can substitute charcoal briquettes for wood; they should be allowed to burn until they are well coated with ash and form a bed of coals about one foot thick.

PREPARING THE MEAT

Beef, pork, lamb, poultry, and wild game should be well thawed, then seasoned. Use any dry rub, herbs, or sauce that you like. Next, wrap different types of meat separately in heavy-duty aluminum foil and place each package of foil-wrapped meat in a damp, pre-soaked, burlap sack. Fold the sack into a package and tie it closed with wire. Leave a loop of wire on top of the bag so it can be removed from the pit with a wire hook or metal rod. If necessary, lightly splash water on the burlap to make sure it is thoroughly damp before placing it in the pit.

FINAL PIT PREPARATION AND COOKING

When the meat packages are ready, smooth out the coals with a shovel or rake and lay a piece of sheet metal over the coals. Pieces of corrugated metal roofing work well for this. The sheet metal should be slightly smaller than the fire pit so that it easily fits into the hole. Don't use painted metal. If you can't find sheet or roofing metal, cover the coals with a thin layer of dirt and lay sheets of heavy-duty aluminum foil on top of that.

Space the meat packages on the metal sheet so they are next to each other but not overlapping or stacked, then lay a second metal sheet (or use several overlapping sheets of aluminum foil) on top of the meat (see photo).

Quickly fill the pit with dirt but be careful the dirt doesn't get in the meat packages and that there are no air pockets. Keep adding dirt and pack it down tightly until no smoke leaks from the pit. When you're done, there should be a mound or layer of soil at least two feet thick covering the food. The soil insulates the pit and prevents air from entering it. The coals consume all of the oxygen remaining in the cooking environment.

In general, allow about 20 minutes of cooking time per pound of beef. You don't need to worry about the food burning since the pit temperature slowly decreases over time. Twelve to fifteen pound roasts will still be pink in doneness in four to six hours; for well-done roasts, cook 30 minutes per pound. Whole chickens and hams take four to six hours and can be left longer~10 or 12 hours if you wish. Dig up the meat just prior to serving and use wire cutters to open the packages.

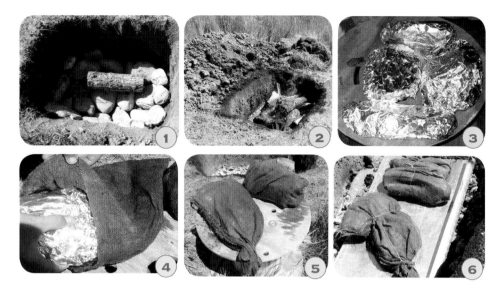

DEEP-PIT BARBECUE INSTRUCTIONS

1. To roast 10-25 pounds of meat, dig a hole three feet deep and at least three feet wide and three feet long. Line the bottom of the pit with a layer of smooth rocks.

2. Start a wood fire in the pit 3 hours or more before you add the meat. Be sure to have plenty of firewood. Charcoal briquettes may be used instead of wood.

3. Wrap different types of meat in separate packages of heavy-duty aluminum foil.

4. Place each package of foil-wrapped meat in a damp, pre-soaked, burlap sack.

5. Fold the sack into a package and tie it closed with wire. Leave a loop of wire on top of the bag so it can be removed from the pit with a wire hook or metal rod. If necessary, lightly splash water on the burlap to make sure it is thoroughly damp before placing it in the pit.

6. Space the meat packages on the metal sheet so they are next to each other but not overlapping or stacked.

7. Place a second metal sheet (or use several overlapping sheets of aluminum foil) on top of the meat packages.

8. Quickly fill the pit with dirt but be careful the dirt doesn't get into the packages.

9. Keep adding dirt and pack it down tightly until no smoke escapes from the pit. When you're done, there should be a mound or layer of soil at least two feet thick covering the food.

10. In general, allow about 20 minutes of cooking time per pound of beef. Whole chickens and hams take four to six hours and can be left up to 10 or 12 hours. You don't need to worry about the food burning since the pit temperature slowly decreases over time. Dig up the meat just prior to serving and use wire cutters to open the packages.

11. Don't want to dig a hole in the ground? You can build an above-ground, deep-pit barbecue with concrete blocks, but you will still need dirt to fill the pit and seal in the heat.

CHAPTER 7

WOOD PLANK COOKERY

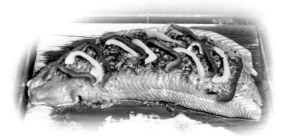

Wood plank cookery is an ancient cooking method that evolved from techniques of native peoples of the Pacific Northwest. Salmon were filleted and roasted on beach-soaked cedar or alder wood sticks and planks placed around a roaring fire. Cooked in this manner, salmon retained its natural juices and was permeated with a rich, smoky flavor.

Modern cooks have adapted this method to an intriguing assortment of foods, including mushrooms, squash, peppers, beef, pork, chicken, shrimp, and scallops. We should mention that barbecuing and smoking methods using soaked hardwood chips or chunks on hot coals are indirect processes that produce a very different result than this direct method. With wood plank cookery, the food cooks directly on the moist wood surface. The delicate wood flavors are transferred directly to the foods and absorbed at lower temperatures. Once you have tasted the deep flavors and savory aromas imparted on basic foods by exotic wood smoke, you will want to cook this way often.

A big advantage of planking is that the plank shields the food from the flame's direct heat, so the food retains its natural texture and succulence. Small food items such as mushrooms and scallops are easy to control and retain their plump shapes and uniformity during cooking.

To get started, go to a lumber store and purchase construction grade, untreated hardwood boards. Various woods can be used. Most hardwood boards are about 3/4 of an inch thick and 8 to 12 inches in width. (Avoid boards more than one inch thick.) Cut the boards into planks 12 to 18 inches long, which are perfect for most plank cooking. You may also find scrap ends of boards in "bone piles" at cabinet and furniture makers. These can generally be had for free or at a greatly reduced price.

Think of the wood as a spice; use your nose and imagination to help determine which wood will imbue that "just right" aromatic smoky flavor to your food. Like the oak essence in a fine chardonnay, the robust wood-smoke aroma blends with the food so you can taste the cedar in salmon, hickory in steaks, and maple in squash.

The best planking woods are maple, oak, hickory, alder, mesquite, western cedar, apple, and peach. You may try other woods, but avoid resinous species like conifers, woods with objectionable odors, or aromatic oily types like sarsaparilla, eucalyptus, and eastern cedar. Here are suggestions for woods and foods that go together very well:

Alder: fish, shellfish
Apple: beef, bratwurst, and pork
Cherry: hamburger, turkey, chicken, and lamb
Cedar, western: fish, and chicken
Hickory: beef, chicken, fish, pork, ribs, sausage, and shellfish
Maple: fish, shellfish
Mesquite: beef, fish, lamb, poultry, and shellfish
Oak: fish, and shellfish
Peach: beef, fish, and poultry
Pecan: beef, chicken, and sausage

To prepare the wood plank, soak it in water for at least four to six hours, and overnight is best. Hardwoods take longer to soak than soft woods. You cannot use dry wood or you'll end up with an

out-of-control flambé. Submerse the wood in a container of water or in a nearby stream. A few rocks placed on top of the board will hold it down for a thorough soaking. If you don't have time to soak the wood for hours, you can speed up the process by soaking the plank in hot water for at least an hour.

When using a container, warm water will speed the soaking process. You can also add spices like sage or basil to make a "tea" to pre-season the board. For special flavors, boards can be soaked in wine, cider, fruit juice, and marinades.

A propane grill is the most convenient way to do plank cooking because it's easy to maintain the high temperature required to heat the board and cook the food. In the field plank cooking works just as well on a portable charcoal grill or the coals of a campfire.

For briquettes or charcoal, be sure to start with plenty of hot coals. Coals should be at least four to six inches in depth to maintain a constant high temperature throughout the cooking process.

For plank cooking over a campfire, you'll need a grate and a cover from an old kettle-style charcoal barbecue. Arrange rocks around the fire pit so that the grill cover rests on the grate with no large gaps or spaces between the cover and the rocks. You want a relatively tight fit to contain the smoke. Evenly spread out the coals and use rocks to support the grill two to four inches above the coals. Be sure to place the plank on the grill and not directly on the coals.

When you're ready to cook, simply place the soaked plank on the grill and heat it for about five minutes or until it starts to crackle and smoke. Next, place the food on the surface of the plank and close the cover. Check the food frequently. A spray bottle of water is handy to extinguish any flames that form along the edge of the board. Cooking times will vary from 12 to 40 minutes depending on the dish and how often you open the cover to check on the food.

If you want to try this process in a more primitive and traditional method without a grill, sharpen one end of a four-foot board to make an oversized stake. Nail a fish fillet to the board and pound the sharpened end into the ground one to two feet away from a roaring alder or cedar wood fire, with the food facing away from the fire. Stoke the fire to keep it hot enough to steadily cook the food. You will both smoke and slow-cook the fish on the wood surface. In addition to stoking the fire up or down, stakes can be tilted towards or away from the fire to regulate heat and cooking times.

Planks can be used for Dutch oven cooking, too. In fact, they are indispensable in many of our recipes. Presoaking the board is not necessary since the plank rests in the bottom of the pot and is bathed in water, basting juices, cider, or other marinade. The food is flavored in wood steam and natural juices.

HEALTHY SEED BURGERS
(6 SERVINGS)

A healthy and tasty version of the standard grilled burger. Extra nutrition at no cost to taste. Everyone loves these.

1 cup bean sprouts
1 medium avocado, peeled and
   coarsely chopped
1 cup Muenster cheese, shredded
1/2 cup plain low fat yogurt
1 T sesame seeds
1 T sunflower seeds
1 T wheat germ
1 t spicy mustard

1 1/2 pounds lean ground beef
1 medium onion, finely chopped
1 large clove garlic, minced
1 t meat tenderizer
1/2 t oregano
1/4 t basil
1/4 t rosemary
1 pinch thyme
6 pita breads, split

1. Thoroughly combine first 8 ingredients; set aside.
2. In a separate bowl, combine remaining ingredients (except pitas).
3. Mix meat and spices thoroughly and shape into 6 patties.
4. Place on presoaked plank on grill for about 3-5 minutes per side or until desired doneness.
5. Warm pita bread.
6. Serve burgers in warmed pita pocket. Top each with bean sprouts and avocado mixture.

Oak Planked New York Steaks (1 STEAK PER SERVING)

Even well done steaks are moist and tender with plank cooking.

thick-cut New York steaks
kosher salt
fresh ground pepper

fresh rosemary sprigs
12-18″ pre-soaked oak plank

1. Pepper New York steaks to taste.
2. Top with fresh rosemary sprigs or any of your favorite herbs and spices.
3. Preheat grill. Place oak (or other wood) plank on grill with high heat and close the lid.
4. When the soaked plank starts to smoke and crackle, place the steaks on the plank.
5. Keep covered, checking periodically for flare-ups, use a spray bottle of water to douse flare-ups. Flip once during cooking, if desired.
6. Salt to taste.
7. Serve when cooked to desired doneness.

CRANBERRY PORK ROAST
(8 SERVINGS)

This wonderful pork roast makes a great substitute for a Thanksgiving turkey.

Western cedar plank
4 pounds boneless pork loin roast
1 large red onion
12 small whole onions
2 t cornstarch
1/4 t cinnamon

1/4 t nutmeg
1/4 t salt
2 T dry sherry
1/2 t grated orange peel
2 T orange juice
1 16-oz. can cranberry sauce with whole
   berries

1. Presoak hardwood plank.
2. Peel small onions and set aside. Cut red onion into 8 wedges.
3. Combine cornstarch, cinnamon, nutmeg, salt, sherry, orange juice and orange peel in a small saucepan.
4. Cook over medium heat, stirring constantly until sauce is thickened. Set aside.
5. Place roast on presoaked Western cedar plank. Keep temperature at a medium heat (about 325º). Cook for 1 hour, watching closely for flare-ups.
6. Add small onions and onion wedges around roast and spoon about 1/2 cup cranberry sauce mixture over the roast and onions.
7. Continue to roast for another 1/2 hour to hour or until meat thermometer is at 160 degrees.
8. Let stand for 10 minutes before slicing. Serve with rest of cranberry sauce.

OAK PLANK GRILLED CHICKEN
BREASTS (4 SERVINGS)

Who would have thought a chicken breast could be this golden-brown yet so moist and tender? The oak and spices make this a mouthwatering dish that deserves a bottle of quality white wine.

4 chicken breasts, skinless
12" to 18" pre-soaked oak plank
1 fresh lime, juiced
1 T Dijon mustard
2 t honey
4-5 cloves of garlic, finely chopped
1 t chili powder
1 pinch cayenne
1 T fresh thyme, minced
1 T balsamic vinegar
Kosher salt
Fresh ground pepper
Tabasco drops to taste

1. Presoak hardwood plank.
2. Prepare marinade by combining lime juice, mustard, honey, garlic, chili powder, cayenne, thyme, vinegar, salt, pepper, and Tabasco.
3. Mix well and pour over chicken breasts; marinate 4 hours in the refrigerator or cooler.
4. Prepare grill to high flame and place plank on grill.
5. When plank begins to crack and smoke, place chicken on top of plank and baste with marinade.
6. Grill, covered, 25-30 minutes, or until juices run clear.
7. Check periodically and use a water spray bottle to douse any flames.

GARLIC SALMON (6-8 SERVINGS)

Garlic and colorful bell peppers complement the plank's rich smoky cedar flavor.

1 large salmon filet
1 18-inch pre-soaked Western
   cedar plank
3 T butter, melted
3 T olive oil
2 T lemon juice
4 T fresh garlic, minced
1 t crushed dried red pepper
1 t fresh tarragon, minced
1/4 t lemon peel, grated
1/4 t chili pepper
1 each red bell pepper and yellow
   bell pepper, sliced
salt & pepper to taste

1. Prepare marinade by combining butter, olive oil, lemon juice, garlic, dried red pepper, tarragon, lemon peel, and chili pepper.
2. Place the salmon, skin side down, on pre-soaked western cedar plank. Brush with the marinade. Top with sliced peppers.
3. Grill, covered, for 20 minutes or until fish flakes with a fork.
4. Check periodically to douse any flames (use spray bottle).
5. Salt and pepper to taste and serve immediately with lemon wedges.

SMOKED VEGETABLES (4 SERVINGS)

hardwood plank, especially oak
1 eggplant, sliced into 1/2 inch
  rounds
2 red bell peppers, halved and
  seeded
2 yellow bell peppers, halved
  and seeded
2 zucchinis, sliced into 1/2 inch
  rounds
2 large onions, peeled and
  sliced into 1/2 inch thick
  round
4 T vegetable oil
1 cup teriyaki sauce

1. Soak oak plank (or hardwood of choice) in water for at least 30 minutes.
2. Preheat grill to high heat. Brush vegetables with oil to coat.
3. Place damp plank on grill. When wood begins to sizzle, place sliced vegetables in a single layer across plank. Cover.
4. Cook vegetables until tender, approximately 10-15 minutes. Vegetables will cook at different rates; remove tender pieces from the plank and keep warm, continue cooking until all are done.

ZUCCHINI OR OTHER SMALL SQUASH (8 SERVINGS)

Use whatever type of squash you like. Squash becomes nicely imbued with the wood smoke flavor.

hardwood plank
4 medium sized fresh zucchini
  and/or other squash
1 T olive oil
2 T fresh, chopped rosemary

1. While wood plank heats, slice squash to 1/2 inch thickness—either in coins or lengthwise in wedges. Small squash can be cut down the middle—grilled in halves.
2. Brush with olive oil and place on sizzling plank.
3. Cover and cook 2 to 3 minutes per side.
4. Sprinkle with fresh rosemary before serving.

CHAPTER 8

DUTCH OVEN COOKERY

I n the 1800s cast iron cook stoves were so heavy and difficult to transport that few settlers owned them. Out of necessity, the Dutch oven was a common household tool of the early pioneers and an integral part of every chuck wagon and mining camp in the Old West.

Efficient, multiple-use stoves eventually became part of homestead kitchens and the use of Dutch ovens greatly diminished. By the 1940s Dutch ovens were almost extinct, but their popularity revived in the 1970s when the "boom for the great outdoors" turned this old-fashioned cookery into new-fashioned cookery. Almost anything you bake at home can be baked in the outdoors with a Dutch oven.

In general, a Dutch oven is a round cast iron or aluminum pot that holds four to eight quarts, has a sturdy wire handle, and usually stands on three short sturdy legs. The lid is made of the same metal with a raised lip around the edge (to hold coals) and a small handle so the lid can be lifted with a gonch hook or tongs. If the oven doesn't have legs, or a rim around the lid, it's not really a Dutch oven.

Original Dutch ovens were all cast iron and heavy. Nowadays you can buy cast aluminum ovens which are one third lighter in weight—something you may want to consider if you are backpacking or carrying it any distance. However, in cooking properties aluminum differs vastly from cast iron. Aluminum conducts heat extremely fast, has a low thermal mass and heat holding capacity, high surface reflectivity, and other chemical properties which make it somewhat difficult and tricky to cook with compared to cast iron.

With its tight fitting lid, the versatile Dutch oven can be used like a pot to cook soups and stews over open flames or partially covered in coals for baking. The entire Dutch oven can be buried in sand or ashes mixed with coals for slow cooking, crock-pot style. The lid can also be flipped over and used as a frying pan. Dutch ovens can be stacked one on top of the other so several dishes can be made simultaneously.

Basic care for a cast-iron Dutch oven is the same as for any cast-iron frying pan. New Dutch ovens are factory coated with wax or grease to protect the metal from rust in shipping and storage. Burn off this coating in an outdoor gas grill until the smoking stops. When the oven cools, thoroughly scrub it with a citrus soap cleanser, rinse with hot water, and immediately towel dry. To season the iron, coat the Dutch oven inside and out with a film of vegetable oil or grease and place it upside down on a grill over the fire. The Dutch oven should be heated until the oil starts to smoke, then left at about 350° until the smoke stops forming. The carbonized oil reacts with the surface of the iron to form a barrier or "patina" that seals and protects the metal from oxidizing and prevents food from sticking to the surface. Once the cast iron is seasoned, never wash with soap or abrasives since they will remove this protective coating. Simply wipe it clean with a damp cloth.

The aluminum Dutch ovens require no initial hot oil treatment but can be a little more difficult to clean. If food is baked on, simply heat water in the oven and, if scraping is necessary, use a wad of aluminum foil or a plastic scour pad.

After cleaning the oven, you should always season it for the next use by wiping a small amount of cooking oil around the bottom sides and in the top. The oil coating keeps rust from forming in the cast iron ovens and prevents surface oxidation on the aluminum ovens.

DUTCH OVEN SIZES

Dutch ovens sizes are coded by number. The #8 oven is 10 inches in diameter and is often used to bake 8-inch pan recipes or single-serving recipes. The #10 oven is 12 inches and is used to bake regular size recipes. Finally, the #12 oven is 14 inches. It is the most common size and is used for large mixes or double recipes. Of course you can place an 8-inch baking pan inside the #12 oven to accommodate single recipes. The #14 oven is 16 inches and is used to bake triple recipes. The size of the oven can help to determine the number of hot coals needed. The bigger the oven, the more coals you need.

FIRE PREPARATION AND COOKING

To prepare the fire for the Dutch oven, you will need a lot of coals. When using wood, start by building a hot fire in a stone-ringed fire pit using sticks of wood four to six inches in diameter. While the fire is burning down to coals (about an hour), dig a separate pit near the fire that is large enough to submerge the Dutch oven onto a bed of hot coals and sandy soil. Plan the hole so you can add an inch or two of coals on top and four inches of coals mixed with sandy soil or ash around the sides of the pot. The cooking temperature is controlled by adding or removing coals around the oven and by carefully using earth and ash to insulate the sides of the oven from the direct heat of the coals. The

Dutch oven can also be placed directly in the fire pit, once the coals are burned down and arranged for secure placement.

If you wish, you may use charcoal briquettes instead of wood coals. Charcoal briquettes are outstanding for Dutch ovens due to their greater density, even shape, and consistent burn rate. They are also easy to handle, burn a long time, and need little refueling. It takes at least 30 minutes for charcoal briquettes to get hot enough to use. Each briquette will add about 35° to a #12, or 14-inch, oven. With this in mind, you can easily judge about how many briquettes you will need, e.g. 10 briquettes x 35 degrees = 350°. In windy or very cold weather, you will need two to eight extra briquettes to counteract the heat lost to the weather.

Whenever possible, pre-heat the Dutch oven by placing a few coals under it before adding your food. Many recipes require you to brown meats or sauté ingredients in the oven before adding other ingredients anyway.

One quarter (or up to one-half on a warm day) of the coals should be underneath the oven with the remaining coals on top of the lid so oven cooks or bakes from the top down. Remember, aluminum conducts heat more efficiently than cast iron so make adjustments accordingly.

After filling the Dutch oven and covering it with coals, do not lift the lid to peek at the food. This allows heat and flavor to escape and the food will to take longer to cook.

Hickory or oak planks can be cut to fit in the bottom of the oven under roasts or other moist cuts of meat where the wood will soak in the juices and marinades and add a distinct aromatic woody flavor to the food. The plank prevents food from sticking to the bottom of the pot and serves as an excellent cutting board as well. An additional benefit is that if the fluids evaporate or the bottom heat is too high, the wood insulates the food from burning, making a low risk cooking method for busy or distracted cooks. Using hardwood planks in the Dutch oven produces vegetable dishes and roasts that are absolutely outstanding.

A great advantage of using a Dutch oven while camping is the ability to slow-cook a main course in an earth-covered pit for four to six hours while you relax or pursue other activities around the camp. The Dutch oven will

become the most versatile cooking implement in your collection. After the great experience of outdoor cooking with Dutch ovens, many people continue to use them for everyday cooking at home, in the kitchen oven or even on the backyard grill.

DUTCH OVEN COAL PLACEMENT TIPS

Baking—On a calm, warm day, keep at least one-half of the coals underneath the oven and the remainder on top of the oven. If it is cool or windy, place three-fourths of the coals on top of the oven with the remainder underneath.

Frying, Boiling and Heating/Reheating Foods—Place all coals under the oven.

Roasting—Place the same amount of coals on the lid and under the oven so the heat comes from the top and bottom evenly.

Stewing and Simmering—Most of the heat should come from the bottom, so place four times as many coals on the bottom as on the lid.

DUTCH OVEN RECIPES

In general you can follow package directions or your own recipes to bake anything in a Dutch oven. The following recipes are some of our favorites. The recipes for fireless cooking in Chapter 14 are easily adapted to the Dutch oven.

BEEF BRISKET (10 SERVINGS)

Start preparation the night before.

6 lb beef brisket
2 t garlic powder (or fresh garlic
    cloves)
1 t black pepper
1 T celery seed
1 10 3/4-oz can condensed
    cream of mushroom soup
1 large onion, sliced
heavy-duty aluminum foil
raised rack for bottom of Dutch
    oven
paprika to taste

1. Place brisket on a large piece of heavy-duty aluminum foil. Season to taste with pepper, garlic powder, and celery seed.
2. If using garlic cloves, cut slits into the brisket and insert a clove or half clove in each slit.
3. Spread soup over brisket and top with onion slices.
4. Wrap brisket tightly in foil and refrigerate overnight.
5. Prior to baking, let brisket stand at room temperature for 1 hour.
6. Place the wrapped brisket into the Dutch oven on a raised wire rack. Bake at 325° for 2 1/2 hours.
7. Uncover brisket, sprinkle with paprika.
8. Return uncovered brisket to oven and bake another 1/2 hour.
9. Slice thinly across grain to serve.

CAMP TACO BAKE (4 SERVINGS)

1 lb ground beef
1/2 cup chopped onion
1/2 cup chopped green pepper
1 pkg taco mix
1/2 cup mayonnaise
3/4 cup water
8 soft corn tortillas
1 cup salsa
1 cup shredded cheddar cheese

1. Brown the beef with the onion and green pepper in the Dutch oven.
2. Add the taco mix, salsa, mayonnaise, and water. Mix well and simmer for 5 minutes.
3. Transfer meat mixture to a bowl. Wipe out Dutch oven.
4. Lightly grease the Dutch oven, then arrange 4 tortillas so they overlap on the bottom.
5. Top tortillas with 1/2 meat mixture, then 1/2 cup cheese.
6. Add another layer of tortillas and top with remaining meat mixture and cheese.
7. Rinse off lid, cover Dutch oven, and simmer over low coals for 15- 20 minutes.
8. Let stand 10-15 minutes before serving.

MONTANA MEATLOAF (6 SERVINGS)

2 lbs ground beef
3 onions, chopped
3 potatoes, with skin, cut in
   1/2 inch cubes
2 carrots, grated
1 cup potato chips, crushed
2/3 cups catsup
2 oz Tabasco sauce

1. Mash ingredients together and place in Dutch oven.
2. Cover and place over small pile of hot coals and cover lid with additional coals.
3. Cook for approximately 30 minutes.

HICKORY PLANKED STEAK
STACKS (4 SERVINGS)

The subtle aroma of hardwood really makes these steaks special and unique. A five-star dish around the campfire!

hickory or oak plank
1 1/2 pound round steak
flour
8 strips bacon, crisp and crumbled
2 T bacon grease
3 medium potatoes, shredded
5 medium carrots, shredded
2 green peppers, sliced
4 onions, sliced
1/2 cup water

1. Cut one hickory or oak plank to drop in the bottom of the Dutch oven.
2. Light 25 briquettes to red-hot.
3. Cut round steak into individual servings, place in a heavy-duty plastic bag with a few teaspoons of flour, and pound steak until thin.
4. Cook bacon in Dutch oven over 10-12 coals, leaving bacon grease on bottom.
5. Brown steak on one side in bacon grease in Dutch oven. Turn and quickly brown other side.
6. Place equal amounts of vegetables on top of each steak, with peppers and onions on top of all.
7. Add salt and pepper if desired.
8. Pour in water, cover, and simmer.
9. Leave 5 coals below and place 12-15 coals on top of oven.
10. Steam until vegetables are tender, about 15-20 minutes.
11. When done, remove steak with vegetables as a single stack.

PLANKED PERFECT ROAST BEEF
(4 SERVINGS)

Want an easy-to-prepare meal with a hickory flavor that will create lasting memories? A planked roast in a Dutch oven is king!

hickory or oak plank cut to fit in
   the bottom of Dutch oven
olive oil
3 lbs eye of round beef roast*
4 potatoes, halved
8 carrots, cut in thirds
3-4 bulbs of garlic
1/2 lb mushrooms, large, whole
2-3 T olive oil
1 T balsamic vinegar
2 sprigs fresh sage
sprig fresh rosemary
spring fresh thyme
1 T kosher salt
1 t fresh ground pepper
1/2 cup water

1. Pour a few tablespoons of olive oil in Dutch oven and heat over coals. Add the roast and brown on all sides.
2. Add water and all vegetable ingredients around roast, wet all with the oil and vinegar and sprinkle spices on top.
3. Roast for 1 hour, 10 minutes for a medium-medium rare roast or roast for 1 hour and 30 minutes for a medium to medium-well roast.

*Wild game can be substituted for beef. If cooking wild game pot roast, add 3 tablespoons white wine vinegar when adding water and spices.

Homestead Style Pork Chops
(4-6 servings)

This is a delectable old family recipe that serves four to six, depending on how much hiking you've been doing! Six small red potatoes can be substituted for the regular potatoes to add color and a crisper flavor.

1 T oil
6 pork chops, 3/4 of an inch thick
3 T butter
4 cups seasoned croutons
1/4 cup water
salt and pepper
3 medium potatoes - quartered, peeled or unpeeled
1 10 1/2-oz can condensed cream of mushroom soup
1/2 cup water
1 T vegetable oil

1. Light 25 briquettes, let burn to red-hot.
2. Preheat Dutch oven.
3. Place 10 coals underneath Dutch oven to sear chops.
3. Place chops in hot Dutch oven with a tablespoon of oil, sprinkling with salt and pepper. Sear chops on both sides.
4. Melt butter in Dutch oven lid.
5. Place croutons in a gallon zipper bag and add melted butter and 1/4 cup water, and mix well.
6. Shape croutons into small balls and lay on top of chops.
7. Place potato quarters around chops.
8. Mix mushroom soup with 1/2 cup water. Pour over top of chops.
9. Cover and place five coals below and 12-15 coals on top and bake for 50-60 minutes.

SAVORY COUNTRY STYLE RIB
(6-8 SERVINGS)

A special thanks to Gail Johnson for this recipe of messy finger-licking ribs! This is definitely the best rib recipe we have tried in the Dutch oven.

3-4 lbs country-style spare ribs
salted water
1 T butter
1/2 cup chopped onion
1/2 cup brown sugar, firmly
    packed
1/2 cup apple cider vinegar
1/4 cup chili sauce
1/2 cup catsup
2 T Worcestershire
1 T lemon juice
1/2 t dry mustard
1 garlic clove, minced

1. Place ribs in Dutch oven. Add salted water to cover.
2. Bring to boil; simmer uncovered for 1 hour or until tender.
3. Drain ribs and transfer to dish and cover.
4. Wipe liquid out of Dutch oven, then melt butter in bottom of oven.
5. Add onions and sauté.
6. Mix remaining ingredients to make sauce.
7. Return ribs to Dutch oven and pour sauce over ribs.
8. Bake on coals at approximately 300° for 30 minutes.

GINGER CHICKEN (4-6 SERVINGS)

This is a very simple recipe to prepare but it will taste like something only a professional chef could have made. Marinate for 4 hours; cook for 1 hour. The Dutch oven does all the hard work.

1 whole chicken (or enough pieces to make the equivalent)
1 T ground ginger or 2 t freshly grated ginger
1 T soy sauce
1/4 cup olive oil

1. Mix ginger, soy sauce, and olive oil in a non-aluminum container or a plastic zipper bag.
2. Add chicken, mix to coat, and marinate for 4 hours.
3. Bake chicken in hot oven for 1 hour.
4. Remove Dutch oven lid and baste frequently with juices and leftover marinade. Do not use any leftover marinade for basting within last 15 minutes of cooking.
5. Let sit 10 minutes before carving and serving.

ROSEMARY GARLIC BRAISED CHICKEN (6 SERVINGS)

This recipe came straight from a family in Italy. This chicken dish is heartier than most and definitely worth preparing in the Dutch oven to achieve the fullest flavor.

1/2 cup olive oil
1 onion, sliced thinly
6 garlic cloves, sliced
2-3 lbs chicken, cut into pieces
salt
fresh ground pepper

1/2 cup flour
1 T tomato paste
1/4 cup – 1/2 cup chicken stock or canned chicken broth
1 T dried rosemary
3/4 cup dry white whine

1. Heat oil in large Dutch oven over medium heat or medium hot coals
2. Add onion and garlic and sauté until soft (about 5 minutes).
3. Remove onion and garlic from oil using a slotted spoon; set aside.
4. Season chicken with salt and fresh ground pepper.
5. Roll chicken in flour to cover. Shake off excess.
6. Brown chicken in Dutch oven. Start with enough chicken (about half) to fit in bottom of pan. When brown, transfer to a plate and brown remaining chicken; set aside.
7. Increase heat; add chicken stock and tomato paste to Dutch oven and bring to a boil, stirring occasionally.
8. Add chicken, sautéed garlic and onion back into Dutch oven. Place a few coals on top the lid and 3 or 4 under the oven and adjust to a low simmering heat by adding or removing coals as needed.
9. Continue cooking for 30 minutes, turning occasionally.
10. After 30 minutes, crumble in rosemary. Cover Dutch oven again and let cook for another 20 minutes or until chicken is tender, adjusting coals as needed to maintain a simmering temperature. Open oven and turn chicken occasionally.
11. When chicken is done, transfer it to a platter, again using slotted spoon to leave sauce in Dutch oven. Cover chicken with foil to keep it warm.
12. Add dry white wine to sauce and bring to a boil in the oven.
13. Pour sauce over chicken and serve.

POACHED ORANGE HALIBUT

(6 SERVINGS)

1 lb halibut belly, cut into 6 pieces
2 qts water
1/2 qt orange juice
1 t garlic powder
1 pinch cayenne pepper
1/4 t ginger powder

1. Place all ingredients except halibut into Dutch oven. Bring to a boil.
2. Once swiftly boiling, add pieces of halibut one at a time. Cover with lid and bring back to a boil.
3. Lower heat to medium, maintaining a gentle boil.
4. Poach for approximately 15 minutes, or until fish flakes.
5. Remove with slotted spoon; scrape off all skin.
6. Serve immediately.

POACHED TROUT (2 SERVINGS)

Catch fish and take them directly to the campfire. Plan one 12-inch fish per person.

2 fresh trout, about 12 inches long, cleaned
3 cups water
1 cup dry white wine
2 T fresh or 1 T dried chives
2 T minced fresh or 2 t dried basil leaves
1 T chopped fresh or 1 t dried dill
1 T chopped fresh rosemary or 1 t dried rosemary
1 T chopped fresh tarragon or 1 t dried tarragon
freshly ground black pepper to taste
1/2 inch by 2 inch strip of lemon peel
3 T butter
lemon wedges, optional garnish
fresh parsley sprigs, optional garnish

1. In large Dutch oven, mix water, wine, herbs, spices, and lemon peel. Set Dutch oven over hot coals and bring liquid to a boil.
2. Lower heat and simmer 10 minutes.
3. Gently add trout to simmering liquid.
4. Partly cover with Dutch oven lid.
5. Continue to simmer for approximately 10 minutes or until fish becomes firm to touch.
6. Using 2 large spoons or other utensils, gently lift trout out and transfer to plates.
7. Mix butter with 1 tablespoon of cooking liquid in separate small bowl.
8. Scoop out as much of the floating spices as you can to add to this mix.
9. Baste fish with butter mixture.
10. Garnish with lemon wedges and parsley sprigs, serve.

ANYTIME BREAKFAST (4 SERVINGS)

You can substitute boxed, dehydrated hash browns for this recipe, just hydrate and drain first. You can also substitute ham or cooked and crumbled ground pork sausage for the bacon.

6 slices bacon
6 eggs
1 small onion, chopped (or 1 T dried minced onion)
1 clove garlic, minced
1 T olive oil
1 small package shredded frozen hash browns
1 cup grated cheddar cheese
salsa, optional

1. Cook bacon in Dutch oven until crisp. Remove bacon and drain fat. Set aside to cool to handle for crumbling.
2. Beat eggs. Add onion and garlic and stir.
2. Spread oil in Dutch oven. Pack hash browns in bottom of oven.
3. Place crumbled bacon on top of hash browns.
4. Pour egg mixture evenly over top.
5. Sprinkle with cheese and bake 30 minutes.
6. Serve with a side of salsa (optional).

CREAMY CHEESE ENCHILADAS
(9 SERVINGS OF 2 ENCHILADAS EACH)

4 cups Monterey Jack, shredded, divided

2 cups cheddar, shredded, divided

1 medium onion, chopped

1 cup sour cream

4 T chopped fresh parsley

18 flour tortillas

1 cup chopped green chilies

3 15-oz cans tomato sauce

1/2 t dried oregano

3 T chili powder

3/4 t ground cumin

1/2 t pepper

2 cloves garlic, finely chopped

1. Grease Dutch oven.
2. Mix Monterey Jack, 1 cup of the cheddar cheese, half of the chopped onion, sour cream, and parsley.
3. Spoon about 1/3–1/2 cup mixture onto each tortilla and then fold tortilla around filling and face seam side down.
4. Mix remaining ingredients except cheese. Pour over enchiladas.
5. Sprinkle with remaining cheese.
6. Bake until hot and bubbly, approximately 30 minutes.

SMOKY HOT BAKED BEANS
(8 SERVINGS)

A wonderful white bean recipe that beats regular baked beans hands down every time. Can be made ahead of time and reheated.

3 1/2 cups (about 1 lb, 7 oz) dried Great Northern white beans, picked over

1 smoked ham hock (about 4 oz)

1/2 t salt

2 cups finely chopped onion

1 1/4 cups commercial barbecue sauce

1/4 cup Dijon-style mustard

2 oz jar salsa

1/2 cup brown sugar, lightly packed

1/4 cup light molasses

1. Place beans in a heavy large Dutch oven.
2. Cover beans with cold water. Add enough to leave an inch of extra water on top.
3. Bring to boil over medium high heat. Remove from heat and let stand until cool, about 1 hour.
4. Drain and rinse beans. Return to same pot. Cover beans again with cold water. Add smoked ham hock and bring to boil over medium-high heat.
5. Reduce heat to low and simmer bean mixture for 20 minutes.
6. Add salt and simmer until beans are tender, about 20 minutes more.
7. Remove ham hock and set aside.
8. Drain beans, reserving 1 1/2 cups cooking liquid. Return beans to Dutch oven.
9. Combine cooked beans, reserved bean liquid, onion, barbecue sauce, mustard, salsa, brown sugar, and molasses in the Dutch oven.
10. Push reserved ham hock into the center of the bean mixture.
11. Set Dutch oven on coals, put on cover, adding coals to top to make a hot oven (about 350°).
12. Cook 1 hour.
13. Uncover and continue baking until mixture is thick; stirring occasionally. This will take about another 40 minutes.
14. Remove ham hock and serve.

VEGETABLES

Many of the following recipes can be made using a cast iron skillet or the lid from a Dutch oven over a campfire or a propane stove.

CHILI CHEESE CORN (8 SERVINGS)

You may want to mix the ingredients before leaving home in order to simplify cooking later.

4 cups fresh corn kernels, or frozen, thawed and drained kernel corn
1 cup grated cheddar cheese
1 8-oz package cream cheese
1 7-oz can diced green chilies
2 t chili powder
2 t ground cumin

1. Preheat coals or oven to 350° F.
2. Lightly oil or grease Dutch oven.
3. Combine ingredients and mix well.
4. Place in Dutch oven, cover with equal number of coals, top and bottom.
5. Bake until bubbling—about 30 minutes.

COUNTRY CHEDDAR POTATOES (6 SERVINGS)

Use a 12-inch Dutch oven for this side dish that's kin to scalloped potatoes.

1/2 lb bacon, diced
1 small onion, diced (or 1 t dried minced onion)
1/2 cup mushrooms, sliced, optional
6 medium-sized red potatoes, sliced about 1/4" thick
salt and fresh ground pepper to taste
1/2 lb sharp cheddar cheese, grated
1/4 cup grated Swiss cheese

1. Fry bacon in Dutch oven. Add onions (and mushrooms) and sauté.
2. Drain all but a tablespoon of bacon grease off and add sliced potatoes.
3. Add salt and pepper to taste. Mix gently.
4. Place eight coals under oven and 14 on the lid. Cook for 35-45 minutes. Check after 35 minutes. Potatoes should be tender when done.
5. Sprinkle grated cheeses evenly and replace the lid, allowing cheese to melt.
6. When cheese is melted into potatoes, they are ready to serve.

JASPER CHEESE BREAD
(10 PEOPLE SERVINGS OR ONE DOG SERVING)

We named this one after a rambunctious puppy, Jasper. Jasper quickly
and quietly stole an entire loaf and devoured it before we could stop him.
Luckily, we had enough ingredients to make a second batch! Jasper was
right; this bread is worth devouring.

4 1/2 cups Bisquick
2 t garlic salt
2 t oregano
2 cups shredded cheddar cheese
1 1/4 cup + 2 T milk or water
1/4 cup butter, melted

1. Mix first 3 ingredients in a gallon zipper bag.
2. Light 15-20 briquettes to red-hot.
3. Preheat Dutch oven with 8-12 coals on top and 5 coals underneath.
4. Lightly oil inside of Dutch oven.
5. Add cheese and milk to dry ingredients; close bag and knead just until
   mixed.
6. Spread mixture evenly in Dutch oven, cover.
7. Add 8 to 12 briquettes to top and leave five coals underneath.
8. Bake for 30 minutes, turning lid of oven a quarter turn every 15 minutes.
9. After baking, brush melted butter over top of bread, sprinkle with a little
   garlic salt if desired. You may also roll out dough and cut into biscuits
   and bake for 20-30 minutes.

SHEEPHERDER'S BREAD

Pioneers, sheepherders, and cowpunchers made sourdough bread because commercial yeast was not available. A fermenting batter containing wild yeasts (Saccharomyces exiguus and Torulopsis holmii) and a bacteria (Lactobacillus sanfrancisco) was used as the dough "starter." Traditionally, miners of the old west would add baking soda and water to the starter and make pancakes. Adding an egg is recommended if making pancakes.

Substitute 2/3 of the white flour with cornmeal, rye, oatmeal, or whole-wheat flour to make different types of bread. Some white flour is necessary to bind the bread together and high-gluten flours are best. The starter is made first, three to four days in advance.

Starter:
  2 cups white flour
  2 T sugar
  warm water

Bread:
  2 T sugar
  1/2 t salt
  1/4 cup shortening
  1 cup warm water
  1 1/2 cup flour

1. Mix flour, sugar, and enough warm water to make a medium thick paste.
2. Pour into a stone or glass jar. Tie a clean, thin cloth over the top, set in a warm place out of the draft.
3. Let paste stand for 3 or 4 days. A hissing sound will come through the cloth and the batter should look bubbly—meaning fermentation has occured.
4. You may reserve 1 cup of the starter and put it in a cool place to use for starting the next batch of sour dough pancakes or bread.
5. To the remainder of the starter, add bread ingredients. Stir well. Continue to add small amounts of flour until stiff dough is formed.
6. Knead well on a lightly floured surface until smooth.
7. Place in a well-greased Dutch oven and let rise about an hour or until doubled.
8. Roll into 1/2 inch thickness and cut with biscuit cutter (top of an opened can works great) or form into loaves.
9. Let rise until doubled again.
10. Bake (very hot oven) for 40-50 minutes for loaves or 20-30 minutes for biscuits.

OLD STYLE RICE PUDDING

1/2 cup long grain white rice (not instant)
4 cups milk
1/2 cup sugar
1/2 t salt
1/2 cup raisins
1/4 t ground nutmeg
1 t lemon zest
1/2 t vanilla
1 egg, lightly beaten, optional

1. Combine uncooked rice, milk, sugar, and salt.
2. Pour into greased Dutch oven.
3. Bake 30 minutes, or until most of liquid is absorbed, at moderate to low heat, stirring frequently.
4. Stir in raisins, nutmeg, lemon zest, and vanilla. Stir in egg (optional).
5. Cover and continue cooking for another 15 minutes.
6. Serve warm or chilled.

CHAPTER 9

STONE SLAB COOKERY

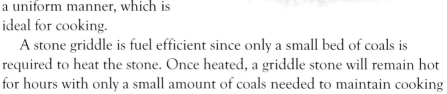

The skill of transferring heat from fire to food by an indirect method was a major step in the evolution of cooking. The use of stone slabs to transfer heat is, most likely, nearly as old as the discovery of fire. A stone slab heated over flames shields the food and distributes the heat in a uniform manner, which is ideal for cooking.

A stone griddle is fuel efficient since only a small bed of coals is required to heat the stone. Once heated, a griddle stone will remain hot for hours with only a small amount of coals needed to maintain cooking temperatures.

Cooking on a stone slab imparts a primitive eloquence to meals over an open campfire. Stone slabs can be used anytime you sauté or fry. Bacon, eggs, pancakes, fish, chops, hamburgers, vegetables, and hash browns can all be cooked simultaneously on a large stone slab.

Stone slabs are inert so they won't impart any flavor into the food. Unlike frying pans, there is no pooling or accumulation of excess fats around the food. Once the food is done, the stone slab can be removed from the fire and used as a hot plate or serving trivet.

GETTING STARTED

Stone slabs for cooking should be siliceous or chiefly quartz and collected away from wet areas. Always avoid sedimentary rocks like shale or slate as they may contain trapped water and can explode when heated. Try to find rocks one- to four-inches thick, a foot or so in length and width, and with at least one smooth surface. A slab less than one-inch thick is prone to cracks and breaking when cold food is placed on the hot surface.

Brush the stone clean and wipe off any soil on the cooking surface with a damp cloth. Slabs should be given a final examination to be sure they are free of major cracks. Place the slab on stable rock supports so that it rests two to four inches above the coals and let it heat evenly for at least an hour. Coat the cooking surface with grease or vegetable oil as you would cast iron.

If you don't want to spend your outdoor time looking for rocks, you can purchase stone slabs at many fireplace and masonry suppliers. These stores generally have several varieties of stone that can be purchased by the pound. An employee can help you select inert rocks composed of granite or basalt, or rocks that predominantly contain quartz

minerals such as quartzite. Inspect the slabs to be sure they are free of major cracks or cavities.

Various sources recommend marble and limestone, and specialty gourmet cooking shops sell marble cooking stones. The caveat is that carbonate minerals in these rocks will chemically react with some cooking ingredients, including wine, lemon or other citrus juice, vinegar, tomato sauce, and certain salts in sauces or marinades. The reaction may influence the food's flavor and other characteristics. You can diminish this effect by first carefully heating and seasoning these stones with cooking oil to form a protective barrier over the entire surface, the same way you would season Dutch ovens.

STONE SLAB RECIPES

Cooking on a slab is much like cooking on a cast iron pan or griddle. Most standard pan-fried recipes work well on a stone stab.

COWBOY CHUCK STEAK
(6-8 SERVINGS)

Start with the foil-wrapped cooking preparation and finish on a stone slab.

Sauce
  1/2 cup honey
  1/4 cup lemon juice
  1/4 cup soy sauce
  2 cloves garlic, crushed
  1/4 t hot pepper sauce

3-4 lb chuck steak
2 T water
1 1/2 T meat tenderizer

1. Blend ingredients for sauce.
2. Moisten steak with water and sprinkle both sides with meat tenderizer.
3. Place steak in the middle of lightly oiled heavy-duty aluminum foil.
4. Cover steaks with 1/2 cup sauce.
5. Double-fold seal the package and place on medium heat coals for 1-2 hours.
6. Remove steak from package and place on preheated stone griddle over coals.
7. Baste with remaining sauce and cook until meat is brown and crusty.

PINWHEELS (4 SERVINGS)

1 1/2 - 2 lb flank steak
1 cup fresh mushrooms, chopped
1 cup fresh spinach, chopped
2 cloves garlic
2 T butter
1/2 t thyme
2 cups herbed stuffing mix
3/4 cup boiling water
1/4 cup melted butter
2 t meat tenderizer

1. Butterfly steak into two thin steaks.
2. Sauté mushrooms, spinach, and garlic in large skillet in 2 tablespoons butter for a couple of minutes.
3. Add thyme. Set aside.
4. In bowl, combine stuffing mix, boiling water and melted butter.
5. Add mushrooms mixture, stir thoroughly, and set aside.
6. Moisten steaks with water. Sprinkle meat tenderizer on both sides and pierce steaks with a fork.
7. Spread half of the stuffing on each steak to within 1 inch of the edges. Roll up, jellyroll style. Secure with toothpicks.
8. Place on preheated stone griddle 8-10 inches from heat, turning frequently, for about 30 minutes or until desired doneness.
9. When done, slice into pinwheels.

Griddled Spicy Double-Thick Pork Chops (12 servings)

You will need to begin this recipe 4 hours before serving.

12 rib pork chops, 1 1/2 inch-thick
9 large garlic cloves
3 qts water
1/2 cup kosher salt
1/4 cup plus 2 T black peppercorns
3/4 cup plus 2 T sugar
1 1/2 T dried thyme, crumbled
1 t whole allspice
1/2 bay leaf
1/2 cup plus 2 tablespoons packed light brown sugar
2 1/2 T ground cumin
1 T kosher salt
1/2 t cayenne pepper

1. Make brine: Lightly mash garlic with flat side of a large heavy knife. In a kettle bring water to a boil with garlic, kosher salt, peppercorns, sugar, thyme, allspice, and bay leaf and simmer 15 minutes. Cool brine completely.
2. Marinate pork chops in brine in plastic bags set in a large bowl. Keep chilled, turning chops once, for 4 hours.
3. Make spice rub: In a small bowl whisk together brown sugar, cumin, kosher salt, and cayenne pepper.
4. Place stone griddle 5 to 6 inches over glowing coals, allow it to thoroughly heat, coat with oil just before cooking.
5. Remove pork chops from brine, discarding brine and any spices still adhering to chops, and pat dry.
6. Season chops with salt and pepper and sprinkle both sides of each chop with about 1/2 tablespoon spice rub, patting it into meat.
7. Grill chops on oiled stone slab 10 to 12 minutes on each side, or until a meat thermometer, diagonally inserted into centers, registers 165 degrees.
8. Remove chops from heat and let stand 5 minutes before serving.

MONTANA-STYLE SWEET AND SOUR PORK (4 SERVINGS)

Marinate the pork three to four hours, and then simmer the marinade in a pot while the tenderloins sizzle on the hot rock slab.

3/4 cup fresh lemon juice
1/2 cup soy sauce
6 T honey
2 small shallots, coarsely chopped
2 large garlic cloves, halved
2 bay leaves, crumbled
2 t salt
2 t pepper
1 t dry mustard
1/2 t ground ginger
4 pork tenderloins, 12 oz each

1. At home, puree the first 10 ingredients in blender to make a marinade.
2. Put two pork tenderloins each into two large sealing plastic bags.
3. Add half of marinade to each bag and seal tightly. Turn to coat.
4. Refrigerate pork in marinade for 3 to 4 hours.
5. Heat rock slab over campfire to medium high heat.
6. Remove pork from marinade and transfer to hot grilling slab.
7. Cook to desired doneness, turning frequently (about 20 minutes).
8. Boil marinade in saucepan until reduced to semi-thick consistency (about 5 minutes).
9. Slice pork in 1/2 inch slices and serve with sauce.

CAJUN BLACKENED TUNA STEAKS
(4 SERVINGS)

Because of the smoke generated by the blackening process, the best place to prepare blackened fish is outdoors, and stone slabs are ideal. The stone gets hot without drying out the fish and the seasonings rapidly sear into a crisp black coating that seals in moisture and spicy flavors. Clean up is a breeze. Just flip over the stone and let the fire take care of that scorched cooking residue.

4 fresh tuna steaks, 1 inch or so in thickness
butter, softened
Cajun seasoning, or blackened-fish seasoning

1. Pre-heat stone griddle on low, stable rock props over a charcoal-rich wood fire, or if you wish, place the slab on the grate in your gas grill and turn the heat to high.
2. Coat each side of the tuna steaks with a thin layer of butter.
3. Sprinkle seasoning over the butter on both sides of the steaks.
4. Cook on very high heat for about 3 to 4 minutes per side or until about medium doneness.

STONE FIRED GOURMET PIZZA

Here's a homemade pizza that will rival the best brick-oven pizza in town! While other stone slabs can be used, a terra cotta tile works best. Season the stone prior to using by coating it with oil, heating it and then allowing it to cool. Do not use detergents on your pizza stone. Clean with cool water only.

For the sake of simplicity, we assume you have dough and sauce ready to go.

Pizza dough

Pizza sauce

Precooked vegetables and/or
   meats, chopped or chunked

Mozzarella Cheese, grated

Parmesan Cheese, grated (optional)

Fresh Basil, chopped (optional)

Extra Flour

Corn Meal

Wood chips or chunks, dry, optional

1. Place the pizza stone in a cold grill. You can use a gas grill, gas with charcoal, straight charcoal or wood. The coals should be at one end of the grill and the pizza stone above and off to the side—not directly above the heat source.
2. Dust the pizza stone with cornmeal before heating. Preheat grill to 500 degrees with the hood closed. Heat stone for approximately one hour.
3. All pizza toppings—meats and veggies, should be cooked and ready to go before rolling out the dough. Uncooked vegetables will make a pizza soggy.
4. While the pizza stone is heating, you can grill peppers, onions, garlic and other ingredients alongside the stone on the grill. Opening and closing the grill will slow the heating process a bit, but roasted veggies are worth it!
5. Using a flour-dusted rolling pin, roll the dough on a floured surface to no more than 1/4 -inch thick and no larger than the width of your pizza stone.
6. Sprinkle a pizza peel/paddle or a cookie sheet with cornmeal before draping the dough disk onto it. Cornmeal helps the pizza slide easily onto the stone.
7. Spread a thin layer of tomato sauce over the dough, top with ingredients, and finish with a layer of mozzarella cheese. Don't overload the pizza or it won't cook evenly or be easy to handle.
8. When the grill has reached 500 degrees, add the wood chunks (oak, cedar or apple). The stone will be extremely hot! Standard grill gloves will likely not be protective. Don't touch the stone!
9. Slide the pizza off the paddle onto the stone. Close the grill lid. After 5 minutes or so, rotate the pizza 180 degress using grilling tongs to ensure even cooking. Continue to cook the pizza for 10-15 minutes or until the crust is browned.
10. With tongs gently work the pizza back onto the pizza paddle or cookie sheet.
11. Sprinkle chopped fresh basil and freshly grated parmesan to your tastes. Fresh cold sliced tomatoes also make a very nice topper.

HOME FRIES WITH WILD MUSHROOMS (6 SERVINGS)

These are wonderful with scrambled eggs or a steak. You can parboil the potatoes a day ahead of time and keep chilled.

3 lbs medium-sized white or Yukon Gold potatoes
4 T butter (1/2 stick), divided
1 T extra virgin olive oil
6 oz fresh shiitake mushrooms
6 oz fresh oyster mushrooms
1/4 cup minced fresh parsley

1. Peel potatoes and cut into 1-inch cubes.
2. Wash mushrooms, remove stems from shiitakes, and quarter any large mushrooms.
3. Cook potatoes in a large pan of boiling salted water until tender (about 10-12 minutes).
4. Drain potatoes and allow cooling.
5. Melt 2 tablespoons of butter with oil on a large stone slab over medium hot coals.
6. Add potatoes and sauté until golden brown. Turn occasionally. Add another tablespoon of butter halfway through cooking.
7. Move potatoes to one side of the stone griddle. On the other side, melt a tablespoon of butter and place mushrooms in the melted butter. Sauté about 6 minutes or until a golden brown.
8. Add sautéed mushrooms and parsley to potatoes and toss to combine.
9. Season with salt and pepper to taste.

APPLE PANCAKES (4 SERVINGS)

Our grandfather made this German recipe with fresh apples from the orchard. The apple pieces add texture and aroma to buttermilk cakes. You need a smooth stone slab for best results.

1 cup apples, unpeeled and cut in pieces
2 cups all purpose flour
1 T baking powder
1 t baking soda
2 t salt
3 T sugar
1 t cinnamon
2 1/4 cups sour milk or buttermilk
2 eggs
6 T butter, melted
vegetable oil

1. Cut unpeeled apples into small pieces.
2. Sift together flour, baking powder, baking soda, salt, sugar, and cinnamon.
3. Beat milk and eggs in a small bowl.
4. Add apples and melted butter.
5. Add the milk mixture to the dry ingredients. Stir well.
6. Preheat stone slab and lightly oil with vegetable oil.
7. Cook as you would ordinary pancakes, browning on both sides.
8. Serve plain or with butter and maple syrup.

Monkey Love Fluffy French Toast (6 servings)

You can make this on the spot, but it turns out better if the dipped bread is allowed to sit overnight. We prepare the bread dip at home and take it to the campsite in a cooler. This dish is guaranteed to wow your fellow campers who can't believe you've cooked something this gourmet on top of a rock.

6 eggs
1 cup milk
1 t vanilla
1 t ground cinnamon
12 slices sourdough French bread (about 1 inch thick)
butter
6 bananas
powdered sugar
1/4 cup slivered almonds, finely chopped

At home:
1. Whisk together eggs, milk, vanilla, and cinnamon until light and frothy.
2. Dip bread slices in egg mixture and place on a greased baking pan.
3. Pour leftover mixture over bread slices.
4. Cover and refrigerate overnight.

At camp:
1. Get a hot fire going and burn it down to a good bed of coals.
2. Preheat rock slab.
3. When rock is hot enough to melt butter, give it a good coating of butter and place bread slices on the rock.
4. Cook until the side is brown, flip, brown other side, cooking about 3 minutes per side.
5. Top with sliced bananas and chopped almonds.
6. Sprinkle with powdered sugar and reap the rewards!

SWEDISH PANCAKES
(MAKES ABOUT A DOZEN, DEPENDING ON SIZE)

Our mother's family emigrated from Sweden to northern Canada in the early 1900s and brought many exceptional recipes with them. Once on a backcountry trip we mentioned that these Swedish pancakes look a lot like French crêpes, but who wants to argue with a cook that has an axe among the kitchen utensils!

3 eggs
1 scant cup flour
1 1/4 cups milk
1 t sugar
1/4 t salt
6 T melted butter (clarified)

1. Prepare hot coals and warm stone griddle over coals until hot.
2. Mix ingredients.
3. Coat hot stone griddle with butter.
4. Drizzle excess butter from stone griddle back into batter and mix quickly. This will help keep the pancakes from sticking and add flavor.
5. Return stone griddle to fire pit.
6. Pour batter by spoonful onto griddle.
7. With back of the spoon spread batter to a thin layer.
8. Pancake will cook quickly.
9. Flip just long enough to brown other side.
10. Serve with butter and sugar and roll up like a tortilla, or serve with berries and cream.

CHAPTER 10

FOIL COOKERY

Many of the recipes in this book, while not specifically calling for the use of aluminum foil, can be readily adapted for foil cooking. Foil is an essential utensil in the outdoors, especially when cooking several foods at the same time. Side dishes can be steamed or baked in their own foil containers separate from the main course. Foil cookery is especially important to the backpacker because it eliminates heavy, bulky cookware. You simply stick a flattened roll or sheet of foil in your backpack and use it to cook a variety of foods, and there are no dishes to wash.

Aluminum foil can be shaped around food and sealed into packets to steam food and hold in cooking juices. Vegetables steamed in foil have a rich, distinct flavor and the package retains vitamins and minerals lost in pot cooking.

Aluminum foil comes in two thicknesses: all-purpose and heavy duty. The heavy-duty foil is best for outdoor cooking because it is less likely to puncture or tear. If lightweight foil is all that's available it should be layered in double or triple thickness.

Successful foil cooking is accomplished by using the "drugstore wrap" to properly seal the package. After wrapping and folding the foil around the food, seal the edges with a double-folded seam. This creates a tight seal that retains steam. Wrap the foil tightly around food that you want to brown, such as meats, or loosely if you want to create a steam package for vegetables. You can also buy foil-cooking bags; these are convenient because you just have to seal one opening.

Foods in foil cook rapidly, and different foods can cooked in sequence, with foods requiring a longer cooking time placed on the fire first. Foil-wrapped foods may be buried in the coals, placed directly atop the coals, or laid on a grill above the coals. Packages buried in coals will cook faster than foods laid on top of or alongside the coals. Packages on the grill will cook slower, more evenly, and are easier to probe and test for doneness. Foods that are normally slow to cook, like potatoes, cook faster when wrapped in heavy foil and buried in the coals.

If a foil package is to be placed directly in the coals, use two layers of foil. This creates a package that is less likely to get punctured, and when you remove the outer wrap, the inside package will be clean and may be used as a plate or serving dish.

Barbecue tongs or long sticks can be used to turn foil packets so all sides cook evenly, and to remove the packets from the fire. Foil cools quickly but a pair of cloth gloves will prevent burned fingers when opening the packages. Tear or cut off the folded ends, or snip the top, and pull open. Use care so that steam from the just-opened foil packs doesn't burn your face or hands.

Cooking in foil is especially useful for those days when everyone, particularly the designated camp cook, is tired and wants a quick, hot, nutritious meal without a lot of
preparation or clean up. Foil cooking is ideal when water or fuel is limited or when you want to pack light.

To prevent unwanted animal visitors in camp, thoroughly burn off any food residue on the foil at the end of the meal. After the fire has cooled, retrieve the foil from the ashes and pack it out.

FOIL COOKING RECIPES

These recipes can be prepared on a home grill, on a grill over a fire, or submerged in hot coals in a campfire

BAKED BEEF FRENCH LOAF
(4-6 SERVINGS)

You can be creative with this fun recipe. Add mushrooms, diced vegetables such as zucchini or carrots, and whatever ingredients you like.

1 large loaf of French bread
1 lb ground beef, extra lean
1 egg, beaten
1 cup cheddar cheese, grated
1/2 cup chopped onion

1/2 cup sliced stuffed green olives, optional
1 cup tomato sauce
1 t salt
1/4 t pepper

1. Cut a slice across the top of the French bread, lengthwise, about 1/2 inch wide.
2. Scoop bread out of crust, leaving a shell. Reserve 1 cup of breadcrumbs.
3. In a bowl, combine 1 cup breadcrumbs with the remaining ingredients.
4. Mix thoroughly and place mixture into bread crust shell.
5. Wrap and seal in large, lightly oiled square of heavy-duty aluminum foil and place package on medium hot coals for about 90 minutes.

SIMPLE POT ROAST (6-8 SERVINGS)

3-4 lbs boneless beef pot roast
1 can condensed cream of mushroom soup
sliced onion or onion powder to taste
salt and pepper to taste

1. Place roast on a large square of heavy-duty foil.
2. Lightly oil the cooking surface of the foil. Place roast on foil, season with salt and pepper, and cover with soup and onion.
3. Double-fold to seal the package and place on medium coals for about 3 hours.
4. Turn the package every 30 minutes or so.
5. Check for doneness after a couple hours of cooking.

STUFFED BURGER SUPREMES
(4 SERVINGS)

These are spectacular! Fast, extremely good, and easy to prepare for hungry campers with a minimum amount of work and clean up. These are best eaten with a fork right out of the foil. Add some foil-wrapped corn on the cob to serve as a side dish (see below).

2 lbs ground beef
salt and pepper to taste
8 deli cheese slices (any kind, 2 slices per burger) or 4 oz crumbled blue cheese
4 tomato slices
4 onion slices
1/2 cup thinly sliced mushrooms

Option: *Dazzle your taste buds by drizzling little drops of Worcestershire, steak, or pepper sauce over the filling before cooking.*

1. Shape burger into eight patties and season with salt and pepper.
2. Place a hamburger patty on a large square of lightly oiled heavy-duty foil.
3. On the patty, place one slice of cheese, onion, tomato, mushrooms, and the 2nd slice of cheese, then place a second patty on top, forming it over the veggie and cheese layers.
4. Pinch together the edges of the meat patties.
5. Mold the meat with your hands so all the filling is completely sealed within the burger shell.
6. Carefully seal the molded burger in foil using a double fold.
7. Repeat steps with the remaining burger patties and ingredients.
8. Submerge the sealed packages in medium-hot coals and bake for about 30 minutes or until done.

BARBECUED FOIL-BAKED CHICKEN DELIGHT (6-9 SERVINGS)

For convenience you can use a commercially bottled barbecue sauce.
We suggest you try the sauce recipe below or use Mom's Barbecue Sauce
(Chapter 3); it's the best!

Sauce:
- 1 onion, sliced
- 1 t salt
- 1 T vinegar
- 1 T Worcestershire sauce
- 1 T sugar
- 1/4 t pepper
- 1/2 cup catsup
- 1/4 cup water

- 1/2 cup flour
- 1 t salt
- dash of pepper
- 1 t paprika
- 3 lb frying chicken, cut up, or pieces of choice
- 1/2 cup butter

1. Combine sauce ingredients into a small saucepan and bring to a boil. Reduce heat and simmer for 10-15 minutes.
2. Mix flour, paprika, salt and pepper in a plastic zipper bag.
3. Toss in chicken pieces, seal bag, and shake to coat chicken with the flour mixture.
4. Place chicken pieces on large lightly oiled squares of heavy-duty aluminum foil, then dot with butter.
5. Pour barbecue sauce over chicken.
6. Seal foil packages and place on medium hot coals for about 1 hour, turning occasionally.

Country Chicken Dinner
(1 serving)

If cooking for more than one person, prepare each serving in a separate foil package. Spice this recipe to your tastes by adding your favorite seasonings.

1 clove garlic, minced
dash of paprika
dash of sage
salt and pepper to taste
1 chicken breast
1 T butter

1 carrot, peeled
1 potato, sliced
1 onion, sliced
4 mushrooms, sliced
2 slices bacon

1. Mix garlic, paprika, sage, salt and pepper. Spread over chicken breast.
2. Place skin side down on large, lightly oiled square of heavy-duty aluminum foil.
3. Dot with butter and place vegetables on top of chicken.
4. Lay bacon strips on top of all.
5. Seal package and place on medium-hot coals for about 1½ hours, turning occasionally.
6. During the last 15 minutes of cooking poke several holes in the foil so the chicken can brown.

FISH A LA ORANGE (1 SERVING)

You can use most any fish fillet (cod, salmon, tuna, etc.) and any seasoning to make a delicious steamed fish dinner. In this recipe, the orange marmalade is a wonderful complement to a light fish like halibut or cod. Almonds add an enjoyable balance of flavor and crunch.

1 fish filet, halibut or other white fish
salt and pepper to taste
2 T orange marmalade
1 T slivered almonds

1. Lightly salt and pepper filet.
2. Spread orange marmalade over top of fish filet.
3. Sprinkle with almond slivers.
4. Make a "fish boat" by loosely wrapping the fish in heavy-duty aluminum foil, leaving extra space for the fish to steam, and double fold the seams.
5. Cook 6 minutes per side.

Carrots (1 serving)

Basically you can prepare peas and green beans the same way.

3 fresh carrots
1 T butter
vegetable oil
salt and pepper to taste

1. Peel and slice carrots into coins.
2. Lightly oil a square of heavy-duty aluminum foil.
3. Place carrots on foil and add butter, salt and pepper.
4. Seal package, place on medium-hot coals for about 15 minutes or until tender.

Corn on the Cob, Steamed (4 servings)

You might not think of parsley and rosemary when someone mentions corn on the cob, but after you try this your thinking may change.

4 ears of corn
2 T butter
4 sprigs fresh parsley
4 sprigs fresh rosemary
salt and pepper to taste

1. Prepare the corn by removing the husks (outside leaves and silky threads).
2. Cut off the stems close to the corn kernels.
3. Cut 4 pieces of foil sufficient to wrap around the corn and place one cob on each.
4. Add a half-tablespoon of butter to each and season with salt and pepper.
5. Place a sprig of parsley and rosemary by each cob.
6. Wrap the foil around the cobs and place the packages on a hot grill for 10 minutes, turning every couple of minutes.
7. Place a cocktail stick or corn holder in each end and serve. (Regular forks work well if you don't have the other items.)

Mushrooms (1 serving)

12 large mushrooms, cleaned
vegetable oil
salt and pepper to taste
butter, optional
minced garlic, optional

1. Dip mushrooms in vegetable oil.
2. Place on a large, lightly oiled square of heavy-duty aluminum foil.
3. Season with salt and pepper.
4. Seal package and place on medium-hot coals for about 15 minutes.
5. To make these more flavorful, add garlic and a couple teaspoons of butter to the package. (Garlic powder also works in place of minced garlic.)

Sweet Potato (1 serving)

1 sweet potato
salt and pepper to taste
dash of nutmeg
1 T butter
1 T brown sugar
vegetable oil

1. Scrub sweet potato. Cut slit in side; be careful not to cut all the way through.
2. Mix salt, pepper, nutmeg, butter and brown sugar together. Press this mixture into the slit.
3. Wrap in lightly oiled square of heavy-duty foil.
4. Seal package and place on medium-hot coals for about 45 minutes or until soft.

BAKED POTATO
(1 SERVING)

1 baking potato
vegetable oil
butter
salt and pepper

1. Scrub baking potato and slice in half.
2. Place on a lightly oiled square of heavy-duty foil.
3. Place a pat of butter on the cut side of each half.
4. Season with salt and pepper to taste.
5. Seal package and place on medium-hot coals for about 45 minutes or until tender, turning about one-third every 15 minutes.

CAMPFIRE BREAD (2 SERVINGS)

1 cup flour
1 t salt
1 T sugar
1 t baking powder

1. Mix ingredients.
2. Slowly add a little water at a time, mixing until you have stiff dough.
3. Pat the dough into a round flat cake.
4. Wrap loosely in foil to allow for the dough to rise.
5. Cook for about 10 minutes.

FOIL-COOKED RICE (6 SERVINGS)

This recipe is a simple, standard side dish, but add raisins, cinnamon, and milk and you have a delicious breakfast cereal, served hot or cold.

2 1/2 cups Minute Rice
2 1/2 cups water
1 T butter
1/4 t salt

1. Tear off two 18-inch square sheets of heavy-duty aluminum foil.
2. Place one sheet of foil on top of the other in a medium size bowl, pressing foil down to shape of bowl.
3. Combine rice, water, butter, and salt and place it in the foil pouch formed in bowl.
4. Fold foil to seal tightly and remove pouch from bowl.
5. Place foil pouch on medium hot coals and cook about 7 minutes, turning occasionally.
6. Open foil and fluff rice.

ROAST BANANA TREAT(1 SERVING)

banana
brown sugar
lemon juice

1. Peel banana and place on a square of heavy-duty aluminum foil.
2. Sprinkle with 1 tablespoon brown sugar and a dash of lemon juice.
3. Seal package and place on medium-hot coals for about 5 minutes.

ROASTED FANCY FRUIT (1 SERVING)

Use peaches, pears, or apples. All fruits turn out quite tasty and make a nice dessert or breakfast item. For a variation, add raisins, cinnamon, and/or chopped nuts.

fruit of choice
butter
brown sugar

1. Peel, halve and remove seeds/core.
2. Melt a couple teaspoons of butter and brush onto the fruit.
3. Place each fruit half, skin side down, on a square of heavy-duty aluminum foil.
4. Sprinkle with brown sugar and dot with an additional dab of butter.
5. Seal package and place on medium-hot coals for about 5 minutes.

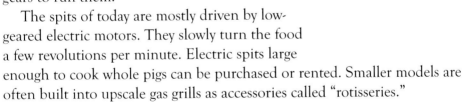

CHAPTER 11

SPIT COOKERY

Spit cookery can be traced back 2,000 years to Asia where ducks were roasted on vertical and horizontal spits. Spit cookery also may have developed independently in other areas. This technique apparently spread westward with nomads, then the Romans popularized it by cooking whole wild boars, goats, deer, and partridge. During medieval times, spits were mechanized and hand turned by turnspits (men or dogs in a treadmill). Spits later became even more sophisticated with some using clock-like gears to run them.

The spits of today are mostly driven by low-geared electric motors. They slowly turn the food a few revolutions per minute. Electric spits large enough to cook whole pigs can be purchased or rented. Smaller models are often built into upscale gas grills as accessories called "rotisseries."

Spit cooking is a barbecue method where large pieces of food are skewered or tied to a wooden or metal shaft that is supported vertically or horizontally over a fire. Small items, such as game birds and fish fillets, can be skewered on sticks with one end of the stick pushed into the ground next to the fire. The food is usually left uncovered but spits have been adapted for use in enclosed "smoky" barbecues. The main advantage of spit or rotisserie cooking is that large pieces of meat or even whole animals can be roasted over a fire in an even manner.

The bane of many campers is that old depiction of a simple spit made with two forked sticks stuck in the ground on opposite sides of the fire. A horizontal stick with the skewered dinner lies across the forks. If you're going to construct a camp spit, don't waste your time trying to build one of these engineering disasters. Just finding two straight sticks topped with usable forks can be an all-day process. Then, after a lot of concentrated effort to stabilize this contraption, the forked-stick spit seldom works properly and most of the time ends up collapsing in the dirt or falling into the fire.

It is much easier to tie three sturdy wooden poles together with rope or wire at one end and make a stable tripod. Suspend the food vertically from the center of the tripod, over the fire. The tripod can be six to eight feet or more in height to keep the legs a safe distance from the fire, and the food can be adjusted to hang the desired cooking distance. Food bundles or meat must be flipped half way through the cooking process to expose the opposite side to the heat of the fire or coals.

If you want a horizontal spit, build two short tripods and place them across from each other outside the fire pit and lay your skewer rod or green pole across the top of them. The height can easily be adjusted higher or lower by moving the tripod legs in or spreading them apart. It takes little effort to assemble these tripod-spit stands in the field and they are both stable and easily adjustable. In addition, pots with wire bales can be suspended over the fire from the center pole, for cooking and boiling water.

The spit must be balanced so the food turns and browns evenly. Try to secure the food on the spit so the food is centered and as compact as possible. Tie on the meat or fasten it with holding forks so it doesn't slip while the rod is turning. Boneless cuts of meat can be molded into a cylinder shape and tied together with heavy cotton string. Wire should be used for more difficult jobs such as securing legs or whole carcasses. Test the operation of the spit to make sure everything is functioning properly before making the fire.

By controlling the size of the fire and the distance of the food from it, cooking temperatures can be adjusted for fast or slow cooking. Ideally, spit-cooked foods should be slowly cooked over coals or in a smoke column, rather than using high heat as with grilling. When cooking over a bed of coals, the rule of thumb is to suspend the meat about eighteen inches over the coals and allow twenty minutes per pound. Moderate coals or a medium gas fire works best for most rotisserie cooking.

Motorized spits or rotisseries are best for large pieces of meat. Many of these units come with counterweights for proper balance. The metal skewer rod doesn't burn and the food doesn't require constant attention since the motor automatically turns the meat. Periodic basting with drippings or sauce will add flavor and form an eye-pleasing glaze or crust.

Some portable spits use 12/24 volt DC motors and can easily be rigged to use car batteries and/or solar PV modules in remote areas. When using a PV module without a battery, the rated amp output of the PV module should be 20 percent greater than the motor's amperage requirements.

BARBECUE SPIT ROAST BEEF
(10-12 SERVINGS)

Use a single cut or a rolled roast. Roast beef on the spit will be tender and juicy.

5-6 lb boneless beef roast
salt to taste
black pepper, freshly ground, to taste
3 cloves garlic, slivered
1 cup safflower, peanut or sesame oil
1/4 cup favorite gourmet steak sauce

1. For a single cut of roast beef, use a narrow thin knife and make 1-inch deep incisions at intervals. Hold incisions open and press salt, pepper, and garlic slivers into the meat.
2. For a rolled roast, untie the butcher's cord and rub salt, pepper and garlic on the inside, roll it back up and retie it.
3. Balance the roast on the spit rod.
4. Begin with a hot fire, high heat, and after the surface of the roast has browned, let temperature reduce to medium-hot.
5. Mix oil and steak sauce. Use this as a basting sauce and baste the roast often as it continues to cook.
6. Use a meat thermometer inserted into the thickest part of meat, without touching spit rod, to test for doneness (see Doneness Chart in Chapter 1 for appropriate temperatures). If you don't have a meat thermometer, the approximate cooking times are: 1/2 hour for rare; 2 hours for medium; 2 1/2 to 3 hours for well done. You may also check doneness by running a skewer or sharp pointed instrument along the spit rod and lifting slightly to observe the color of the internal juice.

ROLLING ROAST FOR ROTISSERIE
(10 SERVINGS)

If the meat is more than one inch thick, make butterfly cuts.

5 lb fully trimmed beef bottom round
2-3 T olive or peanut oil

1. Make a horizontal cut in the center of the slab of meat and slice almost all of the way through it. Open up the meat (now connected at the bottom of the cut) and lay flat. The meat should be of uniform thickness so that the roast will cook evenly.
2. Bacon or oil may be placed on top of leaner cuts of meat, such as game.
3. Tightly roll the meat along the grain so that when sliced after cooking, the cuts will be across the grain.
4. Tie the roast with a 4- to 6-foot wet string or cord.
5. Tie the string around the roast 1 inch from the end and cut off.
6. Repeat loops of string tied around circumference at 1 1/2 inch intervals.
7. Hold the meat firmly and insert spit rod.
8. Brush with oil and set over heat.
9. Check for doneness by inserting a meat thermometer into the thickest part of meat without touching spit rod.

HONEY-GLAZED HAM (10 SERVINGS)

5 lb fully cooked boneless ham
1/2 cup honey
1 T fresh lemon juice
1 t ground cinnamon
1 pinch ground cloves
1/2 cup turbinate sugar or light brown sugar

1. Prepare fire and spit.
2. Place ham on spit and begin cooking. Cook until ham registers 160° when a meat thermometer is inserted into the thickest part (generally, you can estimate about 13-15 minutes per pound).
3. While the ham cooks, mix the honey, lemon juice, cinnamon, and cloves in a small bowl and stir until blended.
4. In the last 30 minutes of cooking, brush the ham with the honey glaze, and then sprinkle sugar crystals evenly over the glaze.
5. Continue rotating and cooking ham.
6. When the ham is done, it will have a beautiful crust. Be careful not to knock off the crust when removing the ham from the spit rod.
7. Cover the ham with aluminum foil and let rest for 10 minutes prior to carving.

JERK PORK (10-15 SERVINGS)

African hunters embarking on long journeys would stuff and coat a whole pig with a spicy seasoned paste and then smoke it over hot coals. Smoking not only cooked the meat but preserved it for eating later on their journeys.

2 onions, chopped
10 green onions with stalks, chopped
6 small green chilies, chopped
thumb size knob of ginger, chopped finely
4 garlic cloves, sliced
1/4 cup allspice

2 bay leaves
sea or kosher salt
black pepper, freshly ground
3 sprigs thyme
3 T olive oil
2 limes, freshly juiced, separated
5-7 lb pork leg roast
2 T whole pimentos

1. Prepare jerk paste by mixing onions, green onions, green chilies, ginger, garlic, allspice, bay leaves, salt, black pepper, thyme, 2 tablespoons olive oil, and 2 tablespoons fresh squeezed lime juice in blender. Blend until a smooth thick paste forms. If you are out in the woods and don't have a blender, do this at home first, or you can be really creative and find rocks to make your own mortar and pedestal for mixing the paste. Reserve remaining juice of this lime.
2. Juice second lime and mix juice with a quart or so of water to wash the pork. Pat dry.
3. Score the pork skin and rub with salt, including into the score marks.
4. Spread the jerk paste evenly over the pork leg, reserving a small amount for basting. Refrigerate or pack in ice in a large cooler and let marinate for 6-8 hours.
5. Place pork leg on spit and cook for 4-5 hours, turning every hour. The pork should be well done or at a minimum temperature of 160°.
6. Add remaining lime juice and another tablespoon of olive oil to reserved paste to make a liquid for basting the pork while cooking.
7. Very important! In the last half hour of cooking, toss 2 tablespoon whole pimentos onto the coals. This will add a delicious smoked pimento flavor to the pork.

Greek Lamb on a Spit
(20-25 servings)

This recipe is for a whole lamb, cleaned, gutted, and well washed.

1 lamb (about 18-20 lbs)
butter
3 lemons, juiced, separated
kosher salt
freshly ground black pepper
olive oil

1. Heat the charcoal and allow the fire to settle. Place the spit in position.
2. Lamb should be washed and drained. Salt and pepper the cavity (inside) of the lamb.
3. Pass the spit rod through the lamb, so that it runs parallel to the backbone.
4. Tie the lamb to the pit rod with thin wire, or a thick strong string, so that the lamb will not slip during roasting.
5. Tie the legs securely to the spit.
6. Sew up the cavity with thick thread so that it will not open while roasting.
7. Baste the lamb with butter and lemon juice. Sprinkle liberally with salt and black pepper.
8. Mix some lemon juice and olive oil and baste the lamb often once it begins to cook. A basting brush works best for this.
9. The lamb must be rotated quickly in the beginning and then slowed down as the meat begins to cook.
10. Continue basting until the lamb is done (about 3 hours) and the exterior is crisp.

CUBAN STYLE SPICY ROTISSERIE CHICKEN (4 SERVINGS)

This zesty chicken will have all your taste buds dancing the salsa! Lime, garlic, and cumin come together for a chicken no one will forget. The chicken should be marinated for four hours and can be started the night before and marinated longer.

1 large whole chicken (broiler-fryer)
1/4 cup fresh lime juice
3 T olive oil
2 large garlic cloves, minced
1 green onion, minced, including
   stalk
1 t lime zest (grated peel)

1 t ground cumin
2 t dried oregano
1 t salt
1/4 teaspoon black pepper, freshly ground
cilantro sprigs
lime slices

1. Wash chicken inside and out and pat dry.
2. Tie the chicken drumsticks together with a thin wire or string.
3. In a large glass bowl, blend together lime juice, olive oil, garlic, onion, lime zest, cumin, oregano, salt, and black pepper. Place chicken in this mixture, turning to coat completely.
4. Cover and refrigerate for 4 hours. During this time, turn the chicken often to rotate the side in the marinade.
5. When ready to cook, pour off marinade and place chicken on spit. Cook for 1 to 1 1/2 or until the leg (or drumstick) easily pulls from the socket. Juice should be clear. (If using a meat thermometer inserted in the thigh, it should register 180°.)
6. After removing chicken from spit, place it on a rack and let it rest for about 10 minutes. Discard strings.
7. Transfer chicken to platter and garnish it with cilantro sprigs and lime slices.

GARLIC CHICKEN (4 SERVINGS)

This is a simple but delicious recipe for the garlic lover.

1 whole fryer or broiler chicken
1/2 cup peeled garlic cloves
salt

black pepper, freshly ground
4 T olive oil

1. Wash the chicken inside and out. Pat dry.
2. Rub chicken with salt and pepper.
3. Place garlic cloves in the cavity of the chicken and close the cavity by stretching skin over it and pinning with toothpicks or sewing with string. Tie legs together.
4. Place chicken on the spit and grill 1 to 1 1/2 hours or until the leg (or drumstick) easily pulls from the socket. Juice should be clear. (If using a meat thermometer inserted in the thigh, it should register 180°.)
5. Baste chicken with olive oil as it turns for an even, tasty, grilled coating.

LIME AND HONEY ROTISSERIE CHICKEN (4 SERVINGS)

This is a rotisserie chicken with lime, honey, and paprika. The end product is completely different than the Cuban chicken with cilantro and lime.

1 whole fryer chicken
1/2 cup oil
2 T honey
2 T lime juice, fresh squeezed
1/2 t paprika
seasoned salt to taste

1. Combine all ingredients, except the chicken, in a saucepan over medium heat.
2. Mix until honey is completely melted and mixture is smooth.
3. Clean and prepare chicken for rotisserie.
3. Baste chicken with sauce and place on rotisserie on preheated grill.
4. Cook for about 35 to 40 minutes at a temperature around 400° F, basting occasionally with sauce. When done, remove from grill and wrap tightly in foil.
5. Let sit for about 15 minutes, then carve and serve.

HERBED TROUT (4 SERVINGS)

This is a fairly simple trout dish, cooked with herb butter. You can use a tripod spit but we suggest vertical skewers next to the fire. This recipe works nicely on a stone slab or a plank as well.

4 fresh trout
4 sprigs fresh rosemary or 1 tablespoon dried
4 T (1/4 cup) butter, softened
leaves of 4 sprigs fresh thyme or 1 1/2 teaspoon dried
4 fresh sage leaves or 1/2 teaspoon dried
1/2 t kosher salt or sea salt
black pepper to taste

1. Clean the trout.
2. Put 1 sprig (or 1/4 t dried) rosemary inside each fish cavity.
3. Chop remaining herbs and add to salt and pepper. Stir this mixture into the softened butter.
4. Coat the fish with the butter mixture, inside and out.
5. Skewer fish and angle over fire, or if using a spit rod, set rod low enough to have a hot temperature.
6. Cook fish 4 to 5 minutes on both sides or until done. When the skin is well browned and flesh is flaking, it is done.

WILD SALMON AND BABY BOK CHOY (6-8 SERVINGS)

A special thanks to Julian Calabrese for sharing this delicious salmon recipe.

2 lb fresh wild salmon filets
sea or kosher salt to taste
black pepper, freshly ground
12 leaves baby bok choy

1 T olive oil
fresh garlic, sliced
1/4 cup chicken broth
juice of 1 lemon

1. Coat salmon with salt and freshly ground black pepper.
2. Place filets on redwood skewers 2.5 to 3 feet in length.
3. Insert skewers in pea gravel, sand, or soft soil near hot coals. (Pea gravel is best because soil or sand may stick to the skewers, and then when you turn the meat by flipping the skewer end for end, dirt can fall onto your food.
4. First place the skin side of the salmon away from the fire. Cook approximately 10 minutes (until done on the surface with a slight crust). After 5 minutes, flip the skewer end for end to heat the other end of the filet, same side. Next, spin skewers so that the opposite sides of fillets are facing the heat. Cook for another 10 minutes, flipping the skewers as before.
5. Sauté baby bok choy in olive oil and garlic slices for 2 minutes over medium-high heat.
6. Deglaze with chicken stock and lemon juice. Cover and let steam to al dente.
7. Remove bok choy and layer with salmon fillet to serve.

CHAPTER 12

REFLECTOR OVEN COOKERY

Reflector ovens were common 200 years ago when open-hearth wood fires were the standard way to cook. The ovens were constructed from sheets of tin placed at angles so they reflected indirect heat from the flames onto the food. The use of reflector ovens gradually declined as efficient cast-iron stoves made their way into kitchens beginning in the 1830s. Highly portable, reflector ovens remained popular with western pioneers until the early 1900s.

The modern reflector oven is an improved version of these relics and has recently been called back to duty by outdoor recreational cooks. Modern reflector ovens are generally constructed of lightweight aluminum sheets that are polished to a mirror-like finish. Angled faces of the oven reflect the fire's heat onto the baking shelf. The temperature of the oven can be regulated by moving it closer to or farther from the flames. This is one of the few cooking techniques where you use high flames instead of coals, so be prepared; the fire will need frequent stoking. We use medium-sized sticks to provide steady, even flames.

While you can fashion a working reflector oven from aluminum foil framed with green sticks of wood, commercial reflector ovens are inexpensive, lightweight, efficient, and conveniently fold flat. There is no

reason not to have one in your camping paraphernalia. Place the oven on a flat, stable surface that has ample room for adjusting it, and as near the fire as you can. If necessary, remove a few rocks from the fire-ring to make a space for the oven. Make sure your baking pan will fit in the oven. Focus the oven's reflective surfaces on the flames. As with any oven, preheat it before placing any food inside. The temperature can be gauged by placing your hand in the oven to feel the radiated warmth.

Use gloves or pads to handle the oven when making adjustments, as it gets hot quickly. While cooking, turn the baking pan front to back at least once so the food cooks evenly. Biscuits or rolls can be turned with tongs to ensure even doneness.

The only caveats to the reflector oven are windy conditions and precipitation. Remember, even though it is an amazing tool, the reflector oven was originally designed for indoor use. To maintain maximum cooking efficiency, remove ash dust and soot accumulations by occasionally wiping the mirrored surfaces of the reflector oven with a non-abrasive damp cloth.

Since you left those bulky pans and Dutch ovens back at base camp, we have selected some splendid recipes that are super matches for the reflector oven. Many of the recipes in this book can be made this way. In fact, just about any recipe that has "bake" or "oven" in the directions can be prepared in these. If you are a beginner, you may want to start with prepared baking mixes and work your way up to meat and fish. If you are backpacking, keep in mind that when a recipe calls for eggs or milk, you may be using the reconstituted equivalents.

ARGENTINE SIRLOIN (4 SERVINGS)

This is great with mashed potatoes or wild rice. It works well for less tender cuts of meats, so feel free to substitute other steak cuts for the sirloin.

1 lb cubed sirloin
salt and pepper to taste
2 T flour
1 1/2 cup red wine
1 t Worcestershire sauce
1 T sugar
1 T curry powder
1/2 t freshly ground ginger
1 T lemon juice

1. Salt and pepper meat.
2. Dredge the meat in flour and place in a lightly oiled baking dish.
3. Mix all remaining ingredients and pour over meat.
4. Bake uncovered in medium-hot (350°) oven until meat is tender.

CHICKEN HASH (12 SERVINGS)

Our grandmother brought back this favorite recipe from a friend in Arizona. You can try game birds in place of chicken, as this recipe works nicely with partridge, pheasant, or any other poultry, and is great way to use leftover meats and poultry. Hash can be partially prepared at home up to a day ahead of time. If doing so, cover and chill hash in one bowl and store chilies-bell pepper mixture in a separate bowl.

2 1/2 lbs new red potatoes
1 large red bell pepper, chopped and seeded
1 cup fresh cilantro, coarsely chopped
2 cups diced cooked chicken
1 large onion, minced
1/4 cup fresh lime juice
3 large jalapeño chilies, seeded and minced
2 large garlic cloves, minced
2 T chicken stock or canned chicken broth
salt and pepper

1. Cook potatoes in a large pot of boiling salted water until just tender. Drain and cool completely, then peel and dice.
2. Mix 1/4 cup bell pepper and 1/4 cup cilantro, potatoes, chicken, onion, lime juice, chilies, garlic, and broth in a large bowl.
3. Season to taste with salt and pepper.
4. Preheat reflector oven.
5. Pour oil into 12-inch diameter skillet.
6. Add hash to pan and press into skillet.
7. Reflector oven will work as a broiler. After the top browns (about 5 minutes), turn browned portions over in sections. Repeat until all of the hash has been turned over.
8. Press into a solid round mound and cook until crusty and brown.
9. Slide hash from skillet onto platter. Sprinkle with rest of bell peppers and cilantro and cut into wedges.

BAKED FISH WITH GARLIC
(2-3 SERVINGS)

Use any firm, white, mild fish—fresh or saltwater. If the fish is frozen, begin by soaking it in 3/4 cup water and 1/4 lemon juice for 10 minutes. This will make a huge difference in the taste of frozen fish!

1 lb fish fillets
salt and pepper to taste
4 T olive oil
1 t minced garlic
1 small dash of oregano
1 lemon, cut into wedges

1. Preheat reflector oven until it feels warm.
2. Pat fish dry, sprinkle with salt, pepper, and place in a greased cooking dish.
3. Mix olive oil, garlic, and oregano and use this to baste the fish.
4. Cover and place in reflector oven, basting occasionally, for 25-30 minutes in a medium hot oven or until fish begins to flake.
5. Serve with fresh lemon wedges.

OPEN-FACED TUNA BAKE
(2 SERVINGS)

2 slices rye or sourdough bread
1 can albacore tuna
2 oz grated cheese
1 chopped celery stalk, optional
1 t lemon juice
1 t chili powder

1. Roll bread flat.
2. Mix other ingredients and spread on bread.
3. Bake in preheated hot reflector oven until cheese is browned and bubbly.

EASY CAMPFIRE BISCUITS
(4 SERVINGS)

These are wonderful to wake up to on a cool morning in the mountains. You can shortcut and use refrigerated dough from the grocery store, but biscuits are easy to make and taste better from scratch!

3 cups flour
6 tablespoons baking powder
½ teaspoon salt
1 cup milk
6 tablespoons oil

1. Set up oven at the campfire to preheat while you prepare the dough.
2. Mix together the flour, baking powder, and salt until well distributed.
3. Add milk and oil and work into a soft dough.
4. Roll out flat on a flour-covered surface. You can use any round can or utensil or glass to roll it out. It's not necessary to bring a rolling pin on your camping trip. You can also just press the dough flat with your palms.
5. Cut out biscuits (we just use an inverted metal cup to cut the dough into circles).
6. Bake until browned. Check for doneness by inserting a knife blade into one of the biscuits. If the biscuits are done, the knife blade will come out clean.

PARMESAN POTATO SPEARS
(4 SERVINGS)

Italian cheeses are great on baked potatoes, adding flavor, color, and crunch!

4 large russet potatoes
1/4 cup olive oil
1 t dried crushed red pepper
salt to taste
fresh ground pepper to taste
1/2 cup freshly grated Parmesan
   cheese
basil, fresh, chopped

1. Cut potatoes into eighths, lengthwise.
2. Preheat reflector oven.
3. Place potatoes in roasting pan. Add oil and red pepper and toss to coat.
4. Season with salt and pepper.
5. Place on shelf in reflector oven and bake until tender on inside and crispy on outside.
6. Turn once during baking (about 1 hour).
7. Sprinkle with Parmesan, basil, and serve.

ROASTED ASPARAGUS WITH LEMON (6 SERVINGS)

Who says you can't be a fine chef with a reflector oven? Surprise your camping friends with this easy, delicious, and nutritious side dish.

3 T fresh lemon juice

1 T extra virgin olive oil

1 t lemon zest (finely grated lemon peel)

36 asparagus spears

salt

pepper, fresh ground

1. Preheat reflector oven to hot (about 450° F).
2. Mix lemon juice, olive oil, and lemon zest in a 15 x 10 x 2 baking pan.
3. Add asparagus and turn to coat with oil mixture.
4. Sprinkle with salt and pepper to taste.
5. Place in reflector oven. Bake until asparagus is tender crisp (about 20 minutes).
6. Serve warm or at ambient temperature.

CORN BREAD (6 SERVINGS)

Corn bread is great for breakfast with butter and syrup, and it is a nice side dish with chilies, soups, and stews. Use an 8-inch square baking pan.

1 cup cornmeal
1 cup all-purpose flour
1 T baking powder
1/2 t salt
4 T sugar
1 cup milk
2 eggs
1/4 cup cooking oil or melted
   shortening

1. Preheat reflector oven until it feels hot (about 425°).
2. Blend all dry ingredients together.
3. Add milk and egg, and stir until batter is smooth.
4. Add shortening and blend.
5. Pour into greased 8-inch square baking dish.
6. Place on reflector oven shelf and bake until top is brown (about 15 minutes).

QUICK COFFEE CAKE (6 SERVINGS)

A tasty breakfast that will provide you with energy for hiking! This is excellent with Stone Boiled Coffee (Chapter 15) on a cool mountain morning.

2 T butter
1/4 cup brown sugar
1 medium can pears, sliced
1 pkg commercial muffin mix

1. Preheat reflector oven until it feels medium hot (about 350°).
2. Melt butter in a 9-inch square pan.
3. Sprinkle with brown sugar and arrange pear slices over the mixture
4. Prepare muffin mix according to package directions
5. Place muffin batter over pears in baking pan.
6. Place baking pan on reflector oven shelf and bake for about 20 to 30 minutes.

SCANDINAVIAN "FRENCH" TOAST
(6 SERVINGS)

This is one of mom's favorites! Again, the Swedes "borrow" from the French like they did with the "Swedish Pancakes" (aka *crêpes*).

3 eggs
1/4 cup milk
1 T sugar
1/4 t cinnamon
1/4 t nutmeg
1 t vegetable oil or melted butter
6 slices of bread

1. Preheat reflector oven until it feels medium hot (about 350°).
2. Beat eggs until fluffy.
3. Add milk, sugar, cinnamon, and nutmeg.
4. Brush cooking surface with oil.
5. Dip one to 2 slices of bread in egg mixture and place in oven on hot cooking surface. Don't dip all the bread at once unless you can cook it all at once. Otherwise, the bread gets too soggy and fragile.
6. Use tongs to flip bread. Each side will need to cook 2 to 3 minutes or until brown.
7. Repeat until all bread is cooked.
8. Serve with berries, syrup, and/or melted butter.

BANANA ORANGE DELIGHT
(8 SERVINGS)

This is a wonderful dessert, but it makes a fabulous breakfast treat as well.

8 ripe bananas
2 oranges, juiced
1/2 cup brown sugar
1 cup shredded coconut
1/2 cup breadcrumbs

1. Preheat reflector oven until it feels warm.
2. Peel bananas and cut in half lengthwise.
3. Arrange halves in greased baking pan.
4. Mix juice of oranges with brown sugar and pour over bananas.
5. Mix coconut with breadcrumbs and sprinkle on top.
6. Place pan on reflector oven shelf and bake until coconut is brown (about 10 minutes).

STICKY BROWN SUGAR CHEWS
(8 SERVINGS)

Brown sugar chews are packed with quick energy and make a great take-along on a long hike.

1 egg
1 cup brown sugar
1 t vanilla
1/2 cup flour
1/4 t soda
1/4 t salt
1 cup chopped walnuts

1. Stir together (do not beat) egg, sugar, and vanilla.
2. Quickly stir in flour, soda, and salt. Add walnuts.
3. Spread in 8-inch square pan and bake in medium hot oven (375°) for 20 minutes.

CHAPTER 13

STEAM PIT COOKERY

Having a large outdoor party, family reunion, or wedding reception? Cook up a celebratory feast with one of these steam pit techniques. Cooking becomes part of the celebration rather than a chore, and the whole process definitely makes a memorable and enjoyable experience for everyone.

Cooking with steam is an efficient method that has been widely in use for thousands of years. Archaeological evidence indicates the Chinese fashioned steamers from ceramic materials more than 3,000 years ago. Primitive earth ovens in other parts of the world include the kup-murri used by Bushmen of Australia and the pachamanca used by pre-Inca Peruvians. Most of these steam pits or "earth ovens" were constructed by digging a fire pit and either lining it with rocks or by adding the rocks directly on the fire. After a good bed of coals is established, the bulk of the fire and loose coals are removed and wet grasses or leaves are placed on top of the hot rocks. The food is placed on the grasses and leaves and then covered with another layer of grass or leaves. Stone "doors" are placed on one end of the pit for easy opening and the pit is covered with soil to insulate it and seal in the steam.

The Hawaiian kalua, the main centerpiece for a lū`au, features whole pigs and vegetables steamed over leaves and hot rocks in a covered pit or "imu." In a similar fashion the Maori of New Zealand build a "hangi." The New England clambake, a steaming technique learned from Native Americans, utilizes wet seaweed placed over hot rocks to produce the steam.

One significant advantage of the steam pit is that heat can be directly transferred to food in the form of radiant heat and steam without smoke, flames, or coals. Foods that cook rapidly, such as clams, lobsters, fish, and vegetables, are ideal for this type of cookery, but many other foods are outstanding when cooked in this manner.

Steaming retains a far higher level of natural flavors and nutrients, as well as vitamins and minerals, than other cooking methods, and since cooking fats and oils are not required, steamed foods are typically lower in fat. Steamed foods get their unique tastes from volatile components in the steam. Flavors from herbs, spices, citrus and smoke are gently distilled onto foods as their vapors travel around the food with the steam.

We have included three steam pit techniques from different regions of the world, with recipes. Note that the basic construction and preparation of these pits are quite similar.

NEW ENGLAND CLAM BAKE
(30 SERVINGS)

This is best on a sandy beach or in sandy soil. This recipe will feed a group of thirty. Bring along lots of napkins and don't forget the shell crackers.

20 lbs clams, in shell, scrubbed clean

10 lbs mussels, cleaned and de-bearded

20 small (1 lb) lobsters

10 lbs cod

5 lbs link pork sausage

5 lbs bratwurst

5 lbs hot dogs

3 lbs sweet onions

20 new potatoes, red or thin-skinned yellow variety, scrubbed

20 ears fresh corn, shucked

20 sweet potatoes, scrubbed

1. Dig a hole in the sand that is about 2 feet wide by 4 feet long and 2 feet deep. Line the pit with smooth rocks and build a fire in the pit. Place more rocks on the fire and keep the fire going so it heats the rocks for 2 to 3 hours.
2. Meanwhile, gather a bushel of seaweed.
3. Wrap cod in damp cheesecloth or foil.
4. Use a shovel and rake to remove burning wood and coals from the hole, then use these tools to arrange the hot stones evenly across the bottom of the pit.
5. Place half a bushel or so of wet seaweed on top of the hot stones.
6. Working quickly, layer the food on top of the seaweed in the following order: clams, mussels, fish, sausage, bratwurst and hot dogs, onions, new potatoes, sweet potatoes, corn, and finally, lobsters.
7. Cover the food with a wet cloth or sheet, then cover this with more seaweed. Place a potato on top. The potato is used as a doneness indicator for the food later on. Splash a little water on the rocks to get some steam going, and then cover the entire pit of food with a wet cloth tarpaulin so the steam is sealed in the pit. Anchor the edges of the tarp with rocks or dirt, but allow a spot where a small amount of steam can escape to relieve any pressure.
8. Let cook for one hour or more. Partially uncover the bake and remove the potato. If it is soft, the bake is done and you can remove the seaweed and cloth covers. Serve with melted butter.

Maori Hangi

Meats for the hangi are generally pork, beef, lamb, and chicken. Vegetables are potatoes, yams or sweet potatoes, sweet corn, and squash. The stuffing is made from breadcrumbs, onions, mixed herbs, and butter.

Use foil to wrap potatoes, corn, and vegetables. Foil can be used to form a tent over meat cuts or in sheets to cover baskets. While foil is commonly used for wrapping foods, leaves are the traditional method. You can use banana leaes or cabbage leaves instead of foil.

Foods are placed in metal baskets or chicken wire folded to form a container. Layering the food in the basket in the proper order is crucial so that everything finishes cooking at the same time. Large cuts of meat or roasts are placed on the bottom with smaller cuts such as chicken on top of that. Potatoes, yams, and squash are next, with corn and cabbage to fill the gaps. Finally, the stuffing is placed on top of the pile. A potato can be placed on top, where it can easily be removed and inspected as an indicator of doneness.

1. Dig a pit roughly 3 feet wide by 5 feet in length and about 18-20 inches in depth. Place the excavated soil in a pile along one side of the pit.
2. Line the pit with smooth, flat stones—preferably of volcanic origin.
3. Arrange kindling in the pit and add logs in a crossed pattern until it reaches the height of the pit. Place more rocks across the top of the wood.
4. Light the fire and allow it to burn 1 1/2 to 2 hours or until all the wood has burned to embers. Use a shovel to reposition any rocks that fall out of the fire. The rocks should be almost red hot.
5. Once the fire has burned down, use shovels and rakes to remove coals and smoking embers so only rocks remain in the hole. Move the coals to a safe area away from the pit and douse with water.
6. Using the rake and shovel, arrange the rocks along the bottom of the pit in an even layer.

7. Place the food basket(s) on the rocks and sprinkle with water. Immediately cover the basket(s) with wet mutton cloth or sheets (or banana leaves), allowing the edges to drape down the hole. Place a potato, which functions as a cooking indicator, on top of the cloth. The potato can be easily tested for doneness throughout the cooking process without disturbing the food baskets.
8. Place wet sacks (or more banana leaves) on top of the sheets but do not let them drape into the hole. The sacks or leaves should form a cover over the hole that is level with the ground.
9. Place a thick layer of dirt on top of the entire covering, sealing off any places where steam escapes.
10. Cooking time for one basket is 2 1/2 to 3 hours, but it can be left for up to 4 hours.
11. Check the potato to see if it is cooked; if the potato is done, then the rest of your food is ready.
12. When the food is done, uncover the dirt from the sacks being careful not to spill any dirt into the basket.
13. Remove the cloth and use the sacks as potholders to remove the hot basket.
14. Arrange food on platters and serve.

Hawaiian Imu Kalua Whole Pig

Whole earth roasted pork is a fun feast for a wedding reception or family reunion. Ti leaves can be obtained from a local florist. If ti leaves aren't available, banana leaves can usually be found at Asian markets or special ordered.

1 whole cleaned and dressed pig
kosher salt
liquid smoke flavoring (optional)
banana or ti leaves or aluminum foil
foil-wrapped bananas, yams, vegetables, and fish or shellfish

1. Dig a hole large enough for the whole pig, roughly 3 feet wide by 5 feet long and 2 feet or so in depth.
2. Line the pit with smooth rocks and stack wood on top of that until the pile is one foot above the top of the pit. Stack extra rocks on the wood to use for placing in the cavity of the pig. Always use rocks collected away from streams or wet areas, otherwise the rocks could burst on heating.
3. Light the fire and allow it to burn down to coals. The fire should burn about 2 hours and the rocks should be bright red-hot.
4. Use a shovel to set aside a few rocks to put in and around the pig. Rake any remaining coals out of the pit leaving the hot rocks bare.
5. Thoroughly cover the surface of the hot rocks with a thick layer (4"-6") of banana or ti leaves, then chicken wire on top of this. Make sure it is big enough to lay the wrapped pig on a flat surface. The ends of the wire should stick 4 inches or so out of the pit, to lift the pig when it is done.
6. Rub the entire surface of the pig, inside and out, with kosher salt.
7. Using a sharp knife, make several 1/2 inch cuts running the length of the pig.
8. Continue to season with salt, pepper, and liquid smoke (optional).
9. Line the stomach cavity of the pig with leaves, and then place some of the hot rocks inside on the leaves. Place a couple of extra-hot rocks next to the thicker portions of the pig (butt and shoulder).

10. Lay more leaves on the chicken wire, then put the pig down on the leaves.
11. Wrap the pig with leaves or foil and tie with wire.
12. Add any other foods such as foil-wrapped bananas, yams, vegetables, and fish or shellfish on the leaves next to the pig. Place more leaves over the food, then cover the leaves with soaked burlap bags, damp sheets, or sheets of metal. Cover the whole pit with dirt so no steam escapes.
13. Relax and forget about the bake for about 45 minutes per pound of pork. This may take 8-10 hours. Check the pit periodically for steam leaks and add more dirt if necessary to plug leaks, since any heat loss will cause a longer cooking time.
14. Using a shovel, carefully remove the dirt, bags, etc., and take out small food items first. Use the wire ends to lift the pig out of the imu.
15. Call everyone to the table. It's going to be grand!

Hawaiian Imu-Kalua Pork
(8-10 servings)

Use the same pit construction as the kalua whole pig, but build a smaller imu.

4-5 lb pork butt roast
2 cups water
2 1/2 T kosher salt
liquid smoke
1 banana leaf (or substitute 4-5 whole bananas, unpeeled, or watercress or big cabbage leaves)
4-6 ti leaves (or substitute aluminum foil)

1. Prepare your roasting pit. Use mesquite wood if available.
2. Trim excess fat from roast.
3. Make several shallow long cuts along the roast's surface or jab repeatedly with a knife to make openings that will allow the smoke to penetrate the meat.
4. Rub the roast with the salt and liquid smoke.
5. Wrap the roast with banana leaf (or watercress or cabbage leaves). If not using a banana leaf, throw 4 or 5 whole bananas on top of the roast.
6. Cut the ribs from the ti leaves and wrap them over the meat—or wrap the entire project in aluminum foil if you don't have ti leaves.
7. Tie securely with twine.
8. Place it in your roasting pit and cover the entire thing with soaked burlap bags, damp sheets or sheets of metal, then cover with enough dirt so no steam escapes.
9. Roast for about 45 minutes per pound of meat. Check the pit periodically for steam leaks, because if you loose heat, the food will take more time to cook.
10. When done, remove leaves and bananas, shred pork, and serve.

CHAPTER 14

FIRELESS COOKERY

Fireless cookery is an extremely efficient primeval cooking art that probably originated in Northern Europe.

Covered pots or kettles of food were heated to boiling on a fire, then placed in insulated "hay-holes" or straw-filled boxes where the food cooked from the residual heat. While this method is briefly mentioned in some older cookbooks, fireless cookery has been pretty much overlooked in the United States since World War II.

Efficient and simple, this method is excellent for camping and other outdoor activities. It uses a minuscule amount of fuel, preserves the food's delicate texture and nutrients, and can be left for long periods without any fire danger or the need for supervision.

The basic principles of fireless cooking are to bring the food just to boiling, drop the heat and simmer for twenty minutes or so, and then place the covered pot in an insulated "nest." Leave the food to cook for four to five hours, or longer, and then serve. If you leave the pot in the cooker so long that the food has cooled, simply bring the pot back to a boil and simmer a few minutes.

The heat retained in the pot slowly cooks the food over a period of several hours and remains hot (145 degrees or more) for up to twelve hours or perhaps longer, depending on the type of insulation and the volume of the cook pot. There is no need to worry about the food burning or overcooking since the retained heat in the cooking pot gradually decreases, allowing the food to gently cook.

This method performs extremely well when you are camping with a single burner gas stove, since you can turn off the stove the moment the pot boils or soon thereafter, conserving fuel. Spaghetti sauces, stews, soups, chili, and many bean and vegetable dishes work well with this method. Many crock-pot recipes cook and taste even better in the fireless cooker.

MAKING A FIRELESS COOKER

Basically all you need is a box or some other cavity that can be lined with an insulating material. A variety of materials and several kinds of containers will work. Adjust the insulation to tightly hold your covered cooking vessel. Use at least four inches of insulation on top, bottom, and around all sides of the pot. Use only pots with tight fitting lids; a Dutch oven or two- to three-quart enameled camp pot is standard.

The type of cooker to build depends on how you will use it and the materials available. If you're camped in the deep woods, you may want to excavate a hole in the ground and line it with sawdust, dry grass, pine needles, bark strips, feathers, cattail fluff, or other materials with insulating properties. Place a folded tarp or sleeping pad over the top of the insulated

hole as a convenient cover. A simmering Dutch oven covered with a towel and carefully wrapped in a sleeping bag and placed in a slightly larger hole in the ground makes an excellent cooker.

Use an old chest cooler lined with pillows or clothing to quickly convert the cooler into an exceptionally efficient cooker that requires no permanent modification. Otherwise, a wooden or cardboard box with a lid can be lined with hay, straw, polyester fiberfill, packing peanuts, or anything with insulating qualities that can be easily shaped around your cooking vessel.

To make a permanent, super-insulated, lightweight, portable cooker, start with any camping cooler large enough to accommodate your cooking pot and four inches of insulation all around it. Line the interior walls and bottom with four- to six-inch thick, foil-faced, fiberglass insulation bats from the local hardware store. Purchase foil-faced fiberglass bats and tape the ends shut or slip the fiberglass bat into an old pillowcase and sew or tape the end shut. Always install the insulation bats with the foil side facing the cooking pot. Shape the insulation to form a nest in the center of the cooler that will hold the cooking pot. Cut one piece of insulation to form a cover over the pot.

FIRELESS COOKER RECIPES

While many foods can be prepared in the fireless cooker, we have selected recipes that are especially good for outdoor cooking. After the initial preparation, the food can be left unattended for long periods with a few, if any, transitional steps during the cooking process.

Foods that take a long time to cook are good choices for fireless cooking. Most crock-pot recipes are quite adaptable to your fireless cooker. Beans, grains, soups, stews, and tough cuts of meat are good foods for all day cooking. Rice cooks exceptionally well in a fireless cooker. (Note: Normally the rule of thumb when cooking rice is to use twice the water volume to rice volume. Because less water is lost as steam with the fireless cooker, less water is needed, so use one-and-a-half times the water volume to rice volume.) Vegetables or foods that can easily over-cook, like pasta, are better cooked the conventional way.

Most stew and soup recipes can be nicely adapted to the fireless cooker. Simply follow your recipe until it lists the cooking time, such as "simmer for 20-30 minutes." Instead, leave it in the fireless cooker for approximately one and a half times the amount of time the original recipe requires. For example, a recipe that calls for simmering for two to three hours would have to be in the fireless cooker for three to four-and-a-half hours. If your daytime adventures keep you gone longer, there is no need to worry. The food won't over-cook or burn since the container temperature is always decreasing.

Most soups and stews are made with beef, chicken, or vegetable stock as a base. Stocks may be prepared in advance (using your fireless cooker or cooking it the conventional way) and even frozen in measured blocks prior to leaving the house. Here are three basic stock recipes to use in all the soups and stews.

BEEF STOCK

3 lbs beef short ribs (or 2-3 lb
   chuck roast)
cooking oil or shortening
2 carrots, cut in thirds
2 onions, cut in half
2-3 stalks of celery with leaves,
   cut in half

1/4 t dried thyme
1 t dried parsley
2 cloves of garlic
2 cups water
salt and pepper

1. Cut chuck roast into chunks or cut ribs apart.
2. Heat oil in stockpot. Add meat to hot oil and brown meat.
3. Add vegetables to pot for the last bit of cooking, long enough to cook them slightly.
4. Add 2 cups of hot water. Stir, scraping loose any browned bits from bottom of pan.
5. Bring to a boil. Skim off any foam.
6. Add water to make pot 2/3 full. Add seasonings. Bring to boil again.
7. Cover, reduce heat, and let simmer for 15 minutes.
8. Quickly, without moving the lid and letting any steam escape, put in the fireless cooker for at least 3 hours. All day is fine.
9. When removed from the cooker, bring to a simmer again for 5 minutes.
10. Adjust seasoning by adding salt and pepper to taste.
11. Strain through a colander. Save meat for hash, tamale pie, etc.
12. Put broth in refrigerator/cooler and let fat congeal on top for easy removal.

CHICKEN STOCK

2 lbs chicken, parts or a whole chicken
1 onion, cut in half
2 stalks celery with leaves, cut in half
1/4 t dry parsley, crumbled

1/4 t thyme leaves, crumbled
1 garlic clove or garlic powder to taste
salt and pepper to taste

Put all ingredients in soup pot.
1. Add about 2 quarts water. Bring to a boil.
2. Boil for 5 minutes and skim off any foam.
3. Reduce heat and simmer with cover on for 10 minutes more.
4. Put in fireless cooker for at least 3 hours.
5. Remove from cooker and adjust seasoning of salt and pepper to taste.
6. Strain stock. Set meat aside to use in soup or other meal.
7. Cool broth and then refrigerate or put in cooler.
8. When chilled, skim off layer of fat. Save chicken fat for cooking, if desired.

VEGETABLE STOCK

You can use many kinds of vegetables except cabbage, broccoli, cauliflower, and Brussels sprouts (these cruciferous vegetables can overpower the flavor of the vegetable stock). The flavor will vary slightly depending on the vegetables. If using tomatoes, go lightly. Some excellent vegetables and vegetable scraps include beets, bell peppers, corn, ears of corn, green beans, green peppers, mushrooms, onions, parsley, peas, garlic, potatoes, scallions, shallots, sweet potatoes, squash, carrots, celery, and fresh basil or other herbs. Fruits such as apples, pears, and pineapple can also be added.

4 cups chopped vegetables, vegetable scraps and/or fruit
1 T black peppercorns
1 whole bay leaf or other spices of preference
1 qt water

1. Place vegetables in a large pot.
2. Add peppercorns and bay leaf. Cover with water. (A good rule of thumb is to have about 50 percent vegetables and 50 percent water, a 1:1 ratio).
3. Cover your ingredients with the water and bring to a boil.
4. Reduce heat and simmer for about an hour.
5. Cool and strain to remove all pieces of vegetables, fruit, or scraps.

Always brown meats on all sides in a frying pan before using in the fireless cooker. Browning produces the desirable meaty flavors and color changes that do not occur at boiling temperatures.

BEEF BARLEY SOUP

1 small onion, chopped
2 t vegetable oil
4 cups beef stock with meat, (see recipe at the beginning of this section)
2 beef bouillon cubes, if desired
Pinch of dried oregano, crumbled
2 garlic cloves or a bit of garlic powder (not salt)
1 bay leaf
1 cup frozen mixed vegetables or 1 cup diced fresh veggies of choice
1 cup potatoes, cubed
1/4 cup barley
1 t Worcestershire sauce

1. Sauté onion in vegetable oil for a few minutes.
2. Add stock with meat, bouillon cubes, oregano, garlic, and bay leaf. Bring to a simmer.
3. Add vegetables and barley. Bring to a simmer again.
4. Simmer 2 minutes and place in cooker for at least an hour.
5. Stir in Worcestershire; remove bay leaf and season to taste.

MONTANA BEEF STEW (4 SERVINGS)

1 1/2 lbs stew meat or beef, cut in cubes
cooking oil
1-2 cloves garlic, or garlic powder to taste
1 large onion, cubed
2 cups potatoes, peeled and cubed
2 carrots, sliced
1/4 cup catsup
pinch of thyme, crumbled
pinch of parsley, crumbled
1/2 cup frozen green peas
salt and pepper
1 t Worcestershire sauce
2 T flour dissolved in 1/3-1/2 cup cold water

1. Heat about 2 tablespoons of cooking oil or shortening in soup pot.
2. Add cubes of beef to brown. Before totally browned, add onion and garlic. Sauté for a few minutes more.
3. Add 3 cups hot water, scraping any browned bits from bottom of pot. Bring to a boil and simmer for 20 minutes.
4. Add potatoes, carrots, catsup, thyme, and parsley. Add water to fill pot 2/3 full. Bring to boil again and simmer 5 more minutes.
5. Put in cooker for a minimum of 3 hours.
6. Remove from cooker and bring to a simmer. Add frozen peas, Worcestershire sauce, and salt and pepper to taste. Add a couple of bouillon cubes if broth does not seem rich enough.
7. Stir in flour/water mixture and continue to heat until mixture thickens. If not thick enough, add in a little more water and flour mix.
8. Stir until thickened.

CHICKEN TACO CHILI (SERVES 8)

Serve topped with shredded Cheddar cheese, a dollop of sour cream, and crushed tortilla chips.

1 white onion, diced
1 16-oz can chili beans
1 15-oz can black beans
1 15-oz can whole kernel corn, drained
1 8-oz can tomato sauce
2 10-oz cans diced tomatoes with green chilies, undrained
1 12-oz can or bottle of beer
1 1.25-oz package of taco seasoning
3 skinless, boneless chicken breasts, cubed, pre-cooked
8 oz cheddar cheese, shredded, optional
1 cup sour cream, optional
tortilla chips, optional

1. Place the onion, beans, corn, tomato sauce, diced tomatoes, and beer in a pot.
2. Add taco seasoning and stir.
3. Add chicken to top. Press chicken down slightly until just covered by chili.
4. Cover and place in fireless cooker for 7 hours.
5. Serve topped with shredded cheddar cheese, a scoop of sour cream, and tortilla chips, if desired.

It's easiest to sort and rinse dried beans the night before. Cover the beans with cold water and let them soak overnight. The best way to cook beans in the fireless cooker is to simmer them for 15 minutes first, then put the pot in the cooker for four to eight hours. Then simmer the beans again for 15 minutes and return the pot to the cooker for another three to eight hours. You likely have been told before that you must change the water and rinse the beans after soaking them. The current school of thought is that flavor and nutrients can leech out of the beans and into the soaking water. It would be a shame to toss flavor and nutrients out! Further, there is no scientific evidence that changing the water cuts down on the beans' gas generation.

You can make bean soup or cook kidney beans for chili or pinto beans for Mexican dishes using this technique. Whatever bean recipe you're fond of, you can adapt to the fireless cooker.

BUFFALO BAKED BEANS

1 qt pea beans
1 t baking soda
3/4 lb salt pork
1 T salt
1/4 t dry mustard
water

1. Clean and sort pea beans, cover with cold water and soak overnight. (You can skip soaking beans but you will need to allow more cooking time if you do.)
2. In the morning, heat slowly to boiling point and add baking soda.
3. Add salt pork, leaving rind exposed. Mix 1 tablespoon salt (if salt pork is not very salty in itself), mustard, and water. Pour over beans.
4. Add enough water to cover beans.
5. Bring to a boil and simmer for 5 minutes.
6. Place in fireless cooker for at least 3 hours.

BASIC BLACK BEAN SOUP

2 cups black beans
1 qt water
1 small onion, chopped
2 stalks celery, chopped
3 T butter, divided
2 t salt
1/4 t dry mustard
cayenne to taste
1 1/2 T flour
2 hard-boiled eggs, sliced
1 lemon, sliced
black pepper to taste

1. Soak beans overnight, drain and add 2 quarts water.
2. Mince the onion and celery and sauté in 1 1/2 T butter; add onion and celery to the beans, and when boiling, put them into a fireless cooker for 8 to 12 hours.
3. Rub the soup through a strainer or puree in a food processor.
4. Add the seasonings and adjust to your taste.
5. Sauté the remaining 1 1/2 tablespoons butter with flour for 2 minutes. Add the resulting roux to the bean mixture, and boil together for 5 minutes.
6. Place sliced eggs and lemon in a soup tureen.
7. Pour soup over the sliced eggs and lemon and serve while hot.

For most types of potatoes (home fries, hash browns, potato salad), simply put the clean potatoes in a heavy pan. Add enough water to cover the potatoes. Bring to a simmer, put lid on tight, and let simmer for two minutes. Then move the pan to your fireless cooker for a minimum of one hour.

For mashed potatoes, peel and cut the potatoes. Bring them to a boil for a minute or two. Place the lid tightly on the pan and put the pan in the fireless cooker for approximately 30 minutes. When done, drain and mash the potatoes, mixing in milk, butter, salt and pepper, as desired. A dash of nutmeg will make them even tastier.

POTATO AND ONION SOUP

2 T butter
2 medium onions, sliced
1 lb peeled and sliced potatoes
1 bay leaf
2 cups milk
2 cups water or stock
salt & pepper
nutmeg

1. Melt butter in pan. Add vegetables, cover, and stew slowly for about 5 minutes or until softened.
2. Add bay leaf, milk, and stock; bring to a boil.
3. Simmer for 2 or 3 minutes, cover and put quickly into the fireless cooker.
4. Leave cooking for at least 1 hour.
5. Remove bay leaf and put soup through a sieve or strainer.
6. Season with salt, pepper, and a grating of fresh nutmeg.

RICE

Vary recipe according to amount needed, using 1 1/2 times as much water as rice. Optional variations: add sautéed vegetables (onion, garlic, celery, peppers), bouillon, and/or spices to the boiling water.

3 cups water
2 cups dry rice, not instant
salt, optional
butter

1. Mix all ingredients and cover with a tight fitting lid. Bring to a boil.
2. Simmer for 5 minutes on a burner or campfire. Don't open the lid as you will lose the necessary steam!
3. Quickly move pan to your fireless cooker.
4. Cook for at least 1 hour.

DESSERT

FRUIT SOUP

Fruit soup was a Christmas tradition at our house. We enjoyed it on Christmas Eve and sometimes spooned it over oatmeal on Christmas morning. It is a Scandinavian favorite as an appetizer or a dessert.

4 cups dried fruit (raisins, currants, apricots, apples, pears, peaches, and prunes)
6 cups (or more) water
4 T small pearl tapioca
1/2 t salt
1 cup sugar
2 cinnamon sticks
1 sliced lemon (or 4 T cider vinegar)

1. Soak all ingredients in the water overnight.
2. In the morning, bring to a boil and transfer to fireless cooker.
3. Let cook for 1 1/2 to 2 hours.

CHAPTER 15

STONE BOILING COOKERY

Stone boiling is one of the most ancient forms of cooking with water. In North America, archaeologists have found evidence of this method in use more than 8,000 years ago, and it has probably been used much longer in other areas of the world. Nomadic tribes used stone boiling long before inventing clay pots or other vessels to hold cooking water.

To boil water and cook, Native Americans dug a small hole in the ground, then lined the hole with either a cleaned hide, a sheet of stomach wall (paunch), or a bladder sack. Flat stones were sometimes placed on the bottom and sides of the hide pot to maintain the pot's shape while the food cooked. Water, meat, and vegetables were placed in the pot. Then, using sticks for tongs, red-hot stones were taken from a fire and dropped into the water to make it boil. Cooled stones were returned to the fire and replaced with hot stones to keep the water boiling or simmering until the meal was cooked.

Native Americans never had to worry about the food being burned by the red-hot rocks. The surface tension of the water causes an insulating steam jacket to form around the hot stone, preventing direct contact with the food. In fact, water can be boiled with hot stones in an ordinary plastic bag without the stones melting the bag, although we don't recommend you cook your foods in a plastic bag or try to hold onto a bag of boiling water!

Boiling stones eventually develop a pattern of stress cracks, or crazing, but they can be reheated and dropped into water up to six or seven times before they begin to break apart. Studies of intact boiling stones from archaeological sites show that boiling stones were carefully selected. Stones were mostly round cobbles with smooth surfaces, mainly composed of quartz or fine-grained "microcrystalline" quartz or quartzite. Stones commonly ranged from "golf ball" to "egg" size, although larger and smaller stones were used since stone mass is directly related to the container size and the total volume of water.

Round stones were preferred over flat or elongated stones because spherical shapes have the highest amount of heating volume with the least amount of surface area. This, along with a smooth surface, allows the transfer of the stone from the coals to the water with a maximum amount of heat delivery and a minimal amount of wood ash or other fire debris. A little ash is good because it provides a source of dietary potassium and the potassium carbonate causes the water to become alkaline, converting saturated and trans fatty acids (the bad fats) into carboxylic acid and glycerol.

You will need a good supply of boiling stones. Ten to 20 pounds are ample, and allow for substitution as you pick and choose among the stones. You don't have to worry about cleaning the rocks prior to use; the fire will burn off any foreign debris and sterilize the stones. Stones heated in coals can reach well over 1800° Fahrenheit.

Stones for boiling should be chiefly composed of quartz or be of volcanic origin like basalt, andesite, quartzite, or granite. Other types of igneous rocks can be used but may not perform as well. Some igneous or metamorphic rocks contain accessory minerals that may leach from the rock at high temperature into the cooking water. This will produce an objectionable metallic taste, so avoid rocks that display "bright pretty colors." You absolutely cannot use rocks of sedimentary origin; they will either explode on heating or shatter from the severe stresses. Always wear protective eyewear, especially if you're unsure of the composition of your rocks. Carbonate-containing rocks like limestone and marble will sublimate at these high temperatures, forming caustic lime salts.

Be fussy when collecting boiling stones; try to find egg-sized, round, fine-grained, rocks with smooth water-worn surfaces composed of chiefly quartz minerals. Remember, they can be heated and submersed in water several times before being discarded so it's worth the effort to find good ones.

If you are unsure of the composition of any boiling stones you have collected, practice first at home. Place selected stones on a cookie sheet and bake in the oven at 200° F for two hours (this will safely remove any water trapped in the rocks), then increase the temperature to 500° and continue to bake for another hour or two. Allow the stones to cool to room temperature and then inspect them. Make a note of the color and composition of any stones that exhibit cracks, peeling, chipping, or flaking and discard those. Lightly tap the remaining rocks with a hammer to ensure their integrity. Rocks tempered in this manner can be safely used for stone boiling. In the field you can temper stones in the same manner by placing them in a covered Dutch oven, first over medium-hot coals and then over hot coals, and run the same tests.

Almost any container that will hold hot liquids without melting can

be used for a boiling container. When backpacking and whitewater rafting, we use heavy-duty foil cooking bags. These bags can be sealed and used for roasting meats and vegetables over coals, or placed upright in a small, shallow hole for stone boiling. Freeze-dried foods can be reconstituted and heated rapidly with a few boiling stones in one of these foil pots.

To begin stone boiling, you will need plenty of coals to heat and reheat the rocks. An oval or elongated fire pit works best. The fire can be forming coals at one end while hot coals and rocks can be raked to the opposite end. Place new wood along the edge of the fire to form new coals. Lump charcoal can be used for the fire in place of wood, but do not use briquettes unless you are certain they are natural charcoal that uses only food starch as the binding agent. Wear gloves and use long-handled tongs to manipulate the hot rocks and coals.

When ready to heat the water, firmly grasp red-hot rocks one at a time with the tongs and lightly tap each stone against a rock. This helps remove any excess ash or debris before plunging the stone into the cooking water.

Stone-heated water boils rapidly and your pot will boil over if too many hot stones are added in rapid succession. Boiling stones will heat the same volume of water several times faster and more evenly than any commercial microwave oven. Use larger stones to start the water boiling, then select smaller stones to maintain a slow boil or simmer.

THE COOKING PROCEDURE

1. Put water in your stone-boiling container (a wooden bucket, metal pot, ceramic vessel, foil bag, or other container of your choice). Leave space to add food and a few boiling stones.
2. Wear gloves and use tongs to select red-hot stones. Tap loose ashes off the stones and drop them into the water.
3. Depending on the amount of water, add enough stones to bring the water to a boil.
4. Add the food and continue to add and replace stones, simmering the food until done.

STONE BOILING RECIPES

For most recipes you will need a 4-quart cooking pot and about ten pounds of boiling stones. The recipes can be adapted for the fireless cooker or Dutch oven, and soup recipes in those chapters can be used for stone boiling.

CAMP COFFEE

The thin, wood-ash residue on the boiling stones actually increases the extraction of caffeine from the coffee beans, so expect an extra jolt from this java!

water
coarse ground coffee
8-10 boiling stones

1. Heat boiling stones to red-hot in coals.
2. Fill pot or pan with water.
3. Submerge hot stones in water until boiling (usually less than a minute).
4. Add coarse ground coffee grounds. For 1 quart of water, use a handful or about 1/4 cup coffee grounds.
5. Let steep for 10-15 minutes or until desired color for strength.
6. Add 1/2 cup cold water to pot to settle coffee grounds to the bottom and serve.

YAUPON TEA (MAKES 2 QUARTS)

10 large stalks fresh mint
2 qts water

1. Heat boiling stones to red-hot in coals.
2. Fill pot or pan with water and add mint.
3. Submerge hot stones in water, bringing slowly to a boil. As soon as water begins to boil, do not add more rocks. Cover pot and let tea steep for 5 minutes.
4. Strain and serve.

BLACKFEET VENISON STEW

Here is an ancient recipe for this cooking method from the Blackfeet Indians in Montana. If you try this recipe using a rawhide pot, be aware that it will shrink dramatically when the water boils.

1 lb fire-dried, smoked venison strips
$1/2$ cup honey or 3 cups birch sap
8 wild onions
10 arrowhead tubers sliced
$1/2$ cup baked camas root
5 sprigs of fresh mint

1. Cut or break the meat into 2-inch chunks.
2. Add water and honey to the skin, and then add meat and remaining ingredients.
3. Drop in hot stones and bring the water to a boil.
4. As the stones cool, replace them with hot stones and maintain a simmer for 45 minutes.
5. Remove all stones and serve.

ISHIYAKI—SEAFOOD SOUP

This is a traditional fish cooking method from Hokkaido, Japan, later modified by the addition or substitution of shellfish and vegetables.

8 raw shrimp (de-veined, shelled)
1/2 lb salmon fillet
1 lb sea bass fillets cut into 1/2 x
   2 inch slices
1 lb yellowtail or mackerel fillets
   cut into 1/2 x 2 inch slices
miso or salt
1 block tofu (cut into 8 equal
   sized cubes)

8 hard shell clams
8 fresh shiitake mushrooms
1/4 lb enoki mushrooms (stems removed)
1 handful of fresh snow peas
2 fresh green leeks (cut into 1/2-inch
   lengths)
large handful of fresh spinach or
   watercress (cut off stems)

1. Pre-bake fish fillets in an oven (Dutch oven or reflector oven).
2. In a wooden bucket, add water and bring to a boil with hot stones.
3. Add miso or salt to taste.
4. Add the fish, shellfish, tofu, and vegetables, then add a few more hot stones so the water boils for a moment to allow the shrimp to cook and the flavor of the ingredients to combine with the soup.
5. Serve immediately—without stones!

SMOKED SALMON SOUP (4 SERVINGS)

This recipe contains a minimum of ingredients, so it is very simple to prepare. You can bulk it up by adding cooked rice and/or additional vegetables.

1 lb sliced smoked salmon, broken
   into bite-sized pieces
1 qt water

3/4 cup baby spinach leaves, cleaned
1/2 t fresh ground pepper

1. Heat water to simmer. Add salmon pieces, simmer for about 15 minutes.
2. Add the spinach and maintain simmer for an additional 5 minutes.
3. Add ground pepper and serve.

CHEESE FONDUE VEGETABLE SOUP (4 SERVINGS)

Use any type of frozen vegetables. It is best to thaw the vegetables before cooking so the water comes to a boil faster. You can also use fresh vegetables but they may take a bit longer to cook.

2 cups chicken broth
1 large bag of frozen mixed vegetables, mostly thawed
1 t coarse salt
1/2 t freshly ground black pepper
1 cup half & half
4 oz Swiss cheese, diced
nutmeg

1. Place chicken broth, vegetables, salt, and pepper in a pot or pan.
2. Add hot stones to bring soup to boil. Keep simmering for 5 minutes.
3. Add half-and-half and a few more stones to bring to near boil or a short boil.
4. Ladle soup into bowls and top off with an ounce of shredded cheese and a sprinkle of nutmeg.

Boiled Corn on the Cobb
(4 servings)

Do not add salt to the water when boiling corn; it makes it tougher. Adding sugar or a splash of milk will make the corn even sweeter. For the best corn, leave the shucks on until you are ready to put the corn in the water. Use a damp paper towel or cloth to remove the silk by grasping the corn by the stalk and brushing the corn silks downward.

4 corn cobs, shucked
20-25 boiling stones about 1 1/2 - 2 inches in diameter
A pot large enough to cover the corn with water
1/4 cup sugar or 1/4 cup milk (optional)

1. Heat the stones in the fire coals to red hot, then add enough stones to the water until it reaches a rolling boil.
2. Add sugar or milk, if desired.
3. Add the corn cobs to the boiling water and add more hot rocks as needed to maintain a steady boil. Leave pot uncovered.
4. Continue boiling 3-4 minutes. The longer corn cooks the softer it gets, so use shorter cooking times for crisper corn.
5. Remove from water to serve. You can leave any extra corn in the hot water and cover the pot until someone is ready for seconds.

Mushroom Soup (6 servings)

1/2 lb mushrooms, washed and coarsely chopped
2 scallions with tops, washed and sliced
6 cups water
3 beef bouillon cubes
1 T butter
1 t salt

1. Place all ingredients into cooking vessel.
2. Add hot rocks to bring to a boil. Allow heat to reduce to simmer.
3. Maintain simmer for 30-40 minutes and serve hot.

John Rittel and Lori Rittel, a brother and sister author duo, grew up on the Blacktail Ranch, a guest ranch in Montana, along with two other siblings, brother Eric, and sister Jeri. The four spent much of their childhood camping outdoors, packing into the backcountry, and even spent a summer living in a teepee in the mountains with their father, Tag Rittel, and a handful of other children from the Dearborn community. Their vast experience outdoors began as children and both continue to enjoy outdoor recreation and outdoor cooking.

John is a geologist, with many published papers in scientific journals. Lori has a master's degree in Food Science and Nutrition, and is a Registered Dietitian. The two decided to bring their experience and unique expertise together to turn their legacy into a book for others to learn from and enjoy.

INDEX TO RECIPES BY FOOD TYPE

Smoked Salmon Soup 189
Wild Salmon and Baby Bok Choy 150

FRUITS & VEGETABLES

Baked Potato 136
Basic Black Bean Soup 179
Boiled Corn on the Cob 191
Buffalo Baked Beans 178
Cheese Fondue Vegetable Soup 190
Chili Cheese Corn 110
Country Cheddar Potatoes 110
Fireless Rice 181
Foil Mushrooms 135
Foil Steamed Corn on the Cob 134
Foil-cooked Rice 137
Foil-wrapped Carrots 134
Grilled Artichokes 72
Grilled Asparagus 72
Grilled Corn on the Cob 73
Grilled Pears 75
Home Fries with Wild Mushrooms 123
Mushroom Soup 191
Parmesan Potato Spears 157
Planked Zucchini or Squash 91
Potato and Onion Soup 180
Roasted Asparagus with Lemon 157
Smoked Vegetables 91
Smoky Hot Baked Beans 109
Squash Kebobs 74
Sweet Potato 135

LAMB

Greek Lamb on a Spit 146
Grilled Lamb 65

MISCELLANEOUS

Anytime Breakfast 107
Blackfeet Venison Stew 188
Camp Coffee 187
Creamy Cheese Enchiladas 108
Maori Hangi 164
Stone Fired Gourmet Pizza 122

Yaupon Tea 187

PORK

Barbecued Pork Spareribs 49
Carne de Chango (Smoked Pork) 50
Cranberry Pork Roast 88
Griddled Spice Double-Thick Pork Chops 119
Grilled Pork Tenderloin 64
Hawaiian Imu-Kalua Pork 168
Hawaiian Imu-Kalua Whole Pig 166
Hickory-Smoked Ribs with Georgia Mop Sauce 52
Homestead Pork Chops 101
Honey-Glazed Ham 144
Jerk Pork 145
Montana Style Sweet & Sour Pork 120
Southern Pulled Pork Shoulder 53

RUBS, SAUCES, & MARINADES

Backyard Barbecue Sauce 38
Basic Pork Rub 29
Beef Stock 173
Caribbean Rub/Paste 29
Charred Chile Salsa 40
Chicken Stock 174
Chili Rub 30
Chimichurri Marinade 34
Choice Chicken Rub 30
Dearborn Rib Rub 31
Diablo Barbecue Sauce 39
Garlic Rub/Paste 31
Hearty Mushroom Sauce 41
Honey Barbecue Sauce 39
Horseradish Rub/Paste 32
Mom's Barbecue Sauce 38
Picante Sauce 41
Red Chili Mustard 42
Roja Coffee Rub 32
Ruby Basin Marinade 35
Sweet-Hot Mustard 42
Tarragon and Lime Supreme Chicken Marinade 34

INDEX TO RECIPES BY COOKING METHOD

BARBECUE

GRILL

DEEP PIT

WOOD PLANK

DUTCH OVEN

STONE SLAB

FOIL

Baked Beef French Loaf 129
Baked Potato 136
Barbecued Foil-Baked Chicken Delight 131
Campfire Bread 137
Country Chicken Dinner 132
Fish a la Orange 133
Foil Carrots 134
Foil Mushrooms 135
Foil Rice 137
Foil Steamed Corn on the Cob 134
Roast Banana Treat 138
Roasted Fancy Fruit 138
Simple Pot Roast 129
Stuffed Burger Supremes 130
Sweet Potato 135

SPIT

Barbecue Spit Roast Beef 142
Cuban Style Spicy Rotisserie Chicken 147
Garlic Chicken 148
Greek Lamb on a Spit 146
Herbed Trout 149
Honey-Glazed Ham 144
Jerk Pork 145
Lime and Honey Rotisserie Chicken 148
Rolling Roast 143
Wild Salmon and Baby Bok Choy 150

REFLECTOR OVEN

Argentine Sirloin 153
Baked Fish with Garlic 155
Banana Orange Delight 160
Chicken Hash 154
Corn Bread 158
Easy Campfire Biscuits 156
Open Faced Tuna Bake 155
Parmesan Potato Spears 157
Quick Coffee Cake 158
Roasted Asparagus with Lemon 157
Scandinavian "French" Toast 159
Sticky Brown Sugar Chews 160

STEAM PIT

Hawaiian Imu-Kalua Pork 168
Hawaiian Imu-Kalua Whole Pig 166
Maori Hangi 164
New England Clam Bake 163

FIRELESS

Basic Black Bean Soup 179
Beef Barley Soup 175
Buffalo Baked Beans 178
Chicken Taco Chile 177
Fireless Rice 181
Fruit Soup 181
Montana Beef Stew 176
Potato and Onion Soup 180

STONE BOILING

Blackfeet Venison Stew 188
Boiled Corn on the Cob 191
Camp Coffee 187
Cheese Fondue Vegetable Soup 190
Ishiyaki—Seafood Soup 189
Mushroom Soup 191
Smoked Salmon Soup 189
Yaupon Tea 187